THE
CHAIN OF
TRADITION
SERIES

**Volume II: Jewish ethics,
philosophy and
mysticism**

Illustrated by

Irwin Rosenhouse

THE
CHAIN OF
TRADITION
SERIES

Jewish ethics, philosophy and mysticism

BY LOUIS JACOBS

Behrman House, Inc.

PUBLISHERS   NEW YORK

for Naomi and Sasson

Published by Behrman House, Inc.,
1261 Broadway, New York, N.Y.

Library of Congress Catalog Card Number: 71-80005

Manufactured in the United States of America

International Standard Book Number: 0-87441-212-9

Introduction

THIS BOOK is divided into three parts: 1) Jewish Ethics, 2) Jewish Philosophy, 3) Jewish Mysticism.

Most of the thinkers represented here belong to the Middle Ages, which in Jewish history must be considered as going to the nineteenth century. Even those who lived at a later period in Jewish history belong in thought to the Middle Ages. The views of modern thinkers are not recorded in these pages, not because they are unimportant but because the book is chiefly concerned with presenting a picture of the older tradition. However, where views are expressed which have parallels in more modern writings the latter are generally referred to in the Comments.

The section on Jewish Ethics, dealing as it does with the patterns of human conduct, is not at all hard to follow. Jewish law sought to create a pattern of living for the Jew. The detailed rules and regulations found in the sources of Jewish law provide a kind of minimum standard for Jewish conduct. But each Jew is expected to rise above the bare minimum and this is where ethics comes in.

The differences between law and ethics in this connection can be briefly stated: 1) Law, as we have just noted, is concerned with minimum standards. Ethics demands something more. For instance, the law forbids the destruction of another's property. Ethics demands that in one's conduct nothing is done which, even indirectly and even in cases not covered by the law, can cause unhappiness and distress to others; 2) Law provides rules for all Jews. Ethics is more individualistic, encouraging each person to realize the best of which he is capable. For instance, the law demands that every Jew must give charity but leaves the amount given to the individual. Ethics demands that each individual should be as generous as his circumstances allow; 3) In law the emphasis is on action. Certain deeds are good, others bad. Ethics, though also concerned with action, tends to place the emphasis on the formation of character. For instance, the law commands men to be generous to one another and not to steal from one another. Ethics seeks to promote the kind of character which has no desire to steal and which automatically responds to cries of help without being ordered so to do; 4) Jewish law is deeply rooted in Jewish history and experience and is addressed primarily, though not exclusively, to Jews. Ethics is more universal. It speaks to the human being with human needs, hopes and strivings so that its appeal is to all men. For instance, one can find laws which have reference only to *Jewish* life e.g. Sabbath observance (which has little meaning for non-Jews except insofar as it reminds humanity of the need for periodic rest and relaxation). But ethical demands such as that men should love truth and pursue justice, awaken an echo in the soul of every man and are, indeed, for the guidance of all men.

The sections on Jewish Philosophy and Mysticism are more difficult both because of the more abstract nature of the subjects discussed and because of the technical language used. An effort has been made to avoid the use of too many technical terms in the translation and where these were unavoidable they have been explained fully in the comments.

Both Jewish law and ethics require a ground or foundation upon which to build. They need a driving force, to vary the metaphor. In order for law to promote the good deed and ethics the good character they must be inspired by a sound philosophy of life. Show me a man's philosophy, said Chesterton, and I'll show you the man. Hence the significance of Jewish philosophy as providing the inspiration for the good life by considering such ultimate questions as: what is life's purpose? why should man be good? what should be man's relationship to God and to his fellow-men? Jewish mysticism is, from this point of view, a branch of Jewish philosophy but with a greater emphasis on individual experience and a more direct awareness of the divine. The mystic seeks to experience in his personal life those ideas about which the philosopher speaks.

There was bound to be some overlapping since philosophy and mysticism frequently consider the same themes and both are concerned, too, with ethical conduct. The thinkers in each section have, however, been chosen as the most typical representatives of that particular type of literature.

When reading a passage in the section on philosophy it is as well to examine carefully all the arguments for and against. The most interesting feature of this type of literature is not so much in the particular views put forward as in the way these are defended. For all that, many of the questions raised are relevant to us today. By understanding the great Jewish thinkers of the past we become better equipped to engage in our own philosophical quest.

When reading a passage in the section on mysticism it is as well to realize that what is generally being put into words is a kind of experience. Since we are not mystics ourselves we have not had these experiences but many people have had at one time or another something not too different from them so that the writings of the mystics do "ring a bell." It might be mentioned here that nowadays there is a good deal of interest in mysticism in some circles. For example there is the fascination which the "mystic East" exercises over some minds and there are people who take drugs to produce hallucinations which, they claim, are similar to mystical experiences. In this connection it is important to realize that the great Jewish mystics did not go out in search of "kicks." Theirs was a severely intellectual approach in which the main thing was to engage in deep contemplation of God in His relationship to the world. Profound thinking about the divine, they taught, might well result in deep ecstasy but it was the thought which mattered, not the resulting sensation. Indeed, one of the most famous of the Jewish mystics declared that if one engaged in contemplation purely for the sake of the resulting sensation one was not a worshiper of God at all, but a self-worshiper! It should always be remembered that the thinkers who appear in these pages belonged to a world different from our own and we should try to understand what they are saying against the background of their times. Yet the quest they engaged in of stating the relevance of Jewish thought and experience to life is still continued by Jewish teachers and must be furthered if Judaism is to make its impact for the ennoblement of human life.

Each section of this book is prefaced by a short Introductory Note. Before reading any particular passage it is advisable to read the Introductory Note to the section in which it occurs.

Jewish ethics

ETHICS IS the science of conduct, of how men should behave. From the earliest times Judaism has had a good deal to say about this aspect of life. Many of the great ideas in Judaism were expressed in legal form and were considered binding upon all Jews. The Ten Commandments are the best-known example of the legal approach.

But in addition to laws binding upon all men, there are the particular requirements made upon Jews because they are Jews. Each person should try to be as good as he possibly can but since no two human beings are alike, their full responsibilities and the development of their character have to be worked out for themselves. The actual *laws* of good behavior are a kind of minimum demand. Over and above these there are numerous teachings which can be applied in particular circumstances but which differ in their application according to the characters and temperaments of different human beings.

For instance, the laws against theft and cheating are for all men. But the teachings about how wrong it is to be quick-tempered or greedy or envious of others will naturally differ in their application. A quiet, gentle person will not need so much to be told of these as would a fiery personality but perhaps the former will benefit more from teachings regarding courage and spiritual ambition. Many ethical and moral teachings of this kind are to be found in the Bible and the Rabbinic literature.

During the Middle Ages and later a whole new type of literature (in Hebrew, the *musar* literature, from a word meaning "instruction" or "reproof"), was developed, based firmly on the classical sources. It is with this type of literature that the following pages are chiefly concerned. This ethical literature examines closely all the ethical teachings of the Bible and the Talmud and presents it in a systematic form so that guidance is readily available on such themes as kindliness, generosity and the cultivation of the wholesome character. The literature serves as a spur to future action. But the readers to whom it was addressed were observant Jews so that the ethical life was not divorced from Jewish law and practice and the whole context of Jewish life. The following selections from that literature demonstrate how great Jewish teachers thought Jewish life should be lived.

Among the particularly outstanding teachers in this field are: Baḥya ibn Pakuda (eleventh century) and Maimonides (1135-1204). Others are: Naḥmanides (1195-1270); Judah the Saint of Regensburg (twelfth-thirteenth centuries), author of the *Sefer Ḥasidim*, "Book of the Saintly"; Jonah ben Abraham of Gerona (Gerondi) (d. 1263), author of *Shaaré Teshuvah*, "Gates of Repentance"; Isaac Aboab (fourteenth century), author of *Menorat Ha-Maor*, "Candelabra of Light" and Moses Ḥayyim Luzzatto (1707-1747), author of *Mesillat Yesharim*, "Path of the Upright." In the nineteenth century the Musar movement was founded by Israel Lipkin of Salant (1810-1883). The followers of this movement laid great stress on sound ethical conduct and produced a number of important works on the subject, although many of the ideas were conveyed orally and have not been written down to this day. Simḥah Züssel of Helm was one of the later leaders of this movement.

If you read the complete works of these men you would see that most of the writers had a strong other-worldly approach to life. That is to say, for them this life is a kind of school in which man is trained to behave well by struggling against evil so that he can go to heaven when he dies (and deserve it). Because of this their work is frequently austere and grim in its outlook and, some would say, not quite to our present-day tastes. It is this which, in part, makes them men of the Middle Ages. From the Renaissance onward men have tried to understand human life much more in terms of this world. But while there is gain in the idea that this life is good in itself, there is still need for the powerful vision of eternal life seen in the Middle Ages. Another feature of life in the Middle Ages was its God-centeredness as opposed to our man-centeredness. The men of the Middle Ages had a strong sense, which we lack, of living to please God. But here, especially, lies the value of these works. They remind modern man in a secular world of how near to God men have been in the past. We are frequently confused in our ethical standards. By reading the work of these men we can learn to see that many of our problems are far from new and that many of the things they said are of value to us today.

CHAPTER 1

BAHYA IBN PAKUDA: ḤOVAT HA-LEVAVOT, "DUTIES OF THE HEART,"
TREATISE III: INTRODUCTION

On gratitude

*How our benefactor's self-interest in doing good
should affect our gratitude to him.*

It will be good to introduce this section of our work by explaining
the different ways in which men do good to one another and their
resulting duty to express gratitude for such benefits. From this we
can move to our duty of praising and thanking God for all the kindnesses and the great goodness He has shown us.

We begin by noting that everyone agrees that we are duty bound
to thank anyone who has been good to us because of his intention
to help us. Even if someone is far from being as generous to us as we
might have wished, because something prevented him from being as
good to us as he intended, we are still obliged to thank him since
we are aware of his good intention and know that he wanted to
help us. If, however, we derived some benefit from a person who
had no intention of helping us, our obligation ceases and we owe
him no thanks.

If we analyze the different ways in which people help one another
we discover that they are not less than five in number. The first way
is like that of a father who is good to his son. The second is like that

of a master who is good to his slave. The third is like that of a rich man who is good to the poor in order to receive reward from Heaven, that is, God. The fourth is like that of men who are good to one another in order to acquire a good name and fame and recompense in this world. The fifth way is like that of the strong man who does good to the weak because he is sorry for him and pained by his condition.

We must now examine the motives of all these types to see whether or not they act for any other reason than to benefit the one who receives the help. Now it is obvious that with regard to the good a father does to his son, the father has his own benefit in mind. For the son is a part of the father and the father's most powerful hopes are centered on his son. You can see that a father feels more for his son than the son himself in providing him with food, drink and clothing and in protecting him from all harm. Since it is natural for parents to be kind to their children and to love them, nothing is too hard for a father to do when the happiness of his child is at stake. Yet despite the fact that he does it as a matter of his nature, both Scripture and common sense make it a duty for the son to serve, honor and respect his parents. As Scripture specifically says: "Ye shall fear every man his father and his mother" (Leviticus 19:3); "Hear, my son, the instruction of thy father and forsake not the teaching of thy mother" (Proverbs 1:8); "A son honoreth his father, and a servant his master" (Malachi 1:6). The son is commanded to give him this respect despite the fact that the father is bound to do whatever he does in this connection by the laws of his nature. His goodness really comes from God and the father is no more than God's instrument.

So, too, with regard to the good a master does to his slave. It is obvious that the master's motive is to protect his investment in the slave since he needs him to work for him. For that he will spend some more of his money in order to protect his money. In spite of this God obligates the slave to work for his master and to be grateful unto him. As it is said: "A son honoreth his father, and a servant his master" (Malachi 1:6).

So, too, with regard to the good a rich man does to the poor in order to receive reward from Heaven. Such a rich man behaves like a smart businessman who gives something small, perishable and unworthy to acquire some great and good benefit which will come to him after a time. His motive is only to adorn his own soul when his life on earth comes to an end. All he has done is to give away something God has deposited with him for the purpose of giving it to whoever deserves it. Yet it is well known that it is right to thank such a man and praise him even though his motive is to adorn his own soul when his life on earth comes to an end. In spite of this he is entitled to praise, as Job said: "The blessing of him that was ready to perish came upon me" (Job 29:13). And Job said further: "If his loins have not blessed me, when he warmed himself with the fleece of my sheep" (Job 31:20).

So, too, with regard to the good men do to one another in order to acquire a good name and fame and recompense in this world. Such good deeds are like someone giving an object of value to someone else to guard for him, or depositing some money with a friend because he fears that he might need it after a time. Even though, as we have said, his motive in doing good to others is really meant to be for his own benefit, nevertheless he is entitled to receive praise and thanks for having done good. As the wise one has said: "Many court the generous man, and everyone is a friend to him that giveth gifts" (Proverbs 19:6). And he also said: "A man's gift maketh room for him, and bringeth him before great men" (Proverbs 18:16).

So, too, with regard to the good a man does to a poor man for whom he feels sorry. His motive is to remove his own pain which comes to him as a result of the anguish and sorrow he feels for the person on whom he has pity. He is like someone who heals a pain he has by giving of that which God has been good enough to give to him. Yet he is not left without praise, as Job said: "Could I see any perish for want of clothing or any poor without covering? Did not his loins bless me, when he warmed himself with the fleece of my sheep?" (Job 31:19-20).

It is obvious from all that we have said that the motive of any man who does good to others is primarily for his own good. He wishes either to acquire for himself an adornment in this world or the next or he desires to remove from himself something painful or he wishes to improve his own property. Despite this we may not withhold praise and thanks, respect, love and gratitude from him for his kindnesses. This is so, despite the fact we have noted that the good such persons give is only loaned to them and they cannot help themselves. Their goodness is not permanent nor is their generosity continuous. Their kindness has in it an element of self-seeking or the desire for self-protection.

How much more, then, is man obliged to serve, praise and thank the Creator of both the goodness itself and the one who bestows it, for His goodness has no limit but is permanent and constant without any self-seeking or self-protecting motives but only an expression of His generosity and lovingkindness toward all mankind!

Baḥya takes the rather cynical view that no human being can do good without at the same time having in his mind the desire to benefit himself. He always "gets something out of it," and self-interest is the basic rule of human nature. For all that, says Baḥya, it is right and proper to thank those from whom we benefit. In that case how much more do we owe thanks to God whose goodness is not for Himself at all but only for us! God can never do good to benefit Himself since God lacks nothing and does not require anything His creatures can give Him.

Some later thinkers have argued that it is incorrect to say, as Baḥya does, that the only human motive for doing good is a selfish one. It can be argued that man has altruistic as well as egotistic instinct and when he does good it can be in response to his altruistic instinct. Ethics must be concerned with man's basic nature and more specifically with the conflicts which arise between his good and evil urges.

On right and wrong

*The difference between not wanting to do wrong
and the exercise of self-control.*

**Some philosophers say of the man who exercises self-control that
although he performs good and worthy deeds he does them while
really desiring and longing to do evil, except that he controls himself. They argue that such a man's deeds are at variance with his
inner character, his lusts and his psychological make-up. Although
he does good it pains and hurts him. The desire and inner nature of
the saintly man, on the other hand, are in full accord with his deeds.
Such a man not only does good but wishes to do so and takes
pleasure in so doing.**

*Maimonides wrote a Commentary to the whole of the Mishnah. The
Eight Chapters are his introduction to that section of the Mishnah
called Ethics of the Fathers. In this book there are collected a number
of typical teachings on ethics from the great Rabbis of old, the
"Fathers." So when Maimonides reached this section he saw fit to
provide a brief introduction to the whole topic of Jewish ethics.
The "philosophers" are Greek and they teach that the truly good
man is not the man who only does good, but the man who
wants to do good.*

**All these philosophers agree that the saintly man is better and more
perfect than the man who has to exercise self-control. To be sure**

they say that in many respects the two are equal. Yet it follows that the man who has to exercise self-control when doing good is inferior to the saintly man since the former really wants to do evil even though in fact he does not do it. His desire to do evil is in itself an unwholesome trait of character.

The superiority of the man who has no desire to do evil over the man who wants to do evil but controls himself is not in the deeds themselves since both types of men do good. The difference between them is that the man who really wishes to do evil suffers from a severe fault of character. There is something unwholesome about him if he wants to do wrong all the time even though, by exercising self-control, he never actually does it.

King Solomon, peace be upon him, said much the same thing: "The soul of the wicked desireth evil" (Proverbs 21:10). Moreover this is what he said with regard to the saintly man who rejoices in doing good, unlike the unrighteous who suffers pain when he does good: "To do justly is joy to the righteous, but ruin to the workers of iniquity" (Proverbs 21:15). It appears that the words of the prophets and the philosophers are in agreement.

Maimonides quotes from the book of Proverbs (attributed to King Solomon) to show that the "prophets" agree with the "philosophers."

When, however, we examine what our sages have to say on this subject we discover that in their opinion the man who longs to sin is worthier and more perfect than the man who has no desire to sin and suffers no pain when he rejects sin. They even went so far as to say that the worthier a man is and the more perfect, the greater will be his desire to sin and his pain in rejecting sin. In this connection they say that the greater the man the more powerful is his evil inclination. Not content with this they say that the reward of the man who exercises self-control is in proportion to the amount of pain the effort at self-control causes him. As they say: "According to the amount of pain involved in doing good so is the reward." Even more than this, they positively commanded a man to have the desire to sin and they warned him never to say that he would not commit this sin because of the laws of his nature even if the Torah had not forbidden it. I refer here to the passage: "Rabban Simeon ben

Gamaliel said: A man should not say: It is impossible for me to eat milk and meat together, it is impossible for me to wear garments of mixed kinds, it is impossible for me to have a forbidden sexual union. But he should say: It is quite possible for me, but what can I do if my Father in Heaven has commanded me not to do it."

Maimonides now points to a contradiction. The sages (Rabbis) appear to say the exact opposite, that the better man is the one who wants to do wrong but controls himself. For the examples quoted by Rabban Simeon ben Gamaliel (2nd century) see Exodus 23:19 (which the Rabbis interpret as forbidding the eating of any mixture of milk and meat); Leviticus 19:19; and Leviticus 18.

Now, at first glance, it would seem that the plain meaning of the two sets of sayings is that they are in flat contradiction. This is not so, however, but both are true and there is no disagreement between them at all. The evils of which the philosophers are thinking, when they declare that one who has no desire for them is superior to one who desires them but controls himself, are evils acknowledged as such by all men, such as murder, theft, robbery, cheating, hurting someone who does not deserve it, ingratitude, insulting father and mother and so forth. These are the kind of commandments regarding which our sages of blessed memory say that even if they were not found in Scripture it would have been necessary to declare them to be binding laws. Some of the later thinkers, afflicted with the malady of the Mutakallimun, call these "rational precepts." There is no doubt that there is something unhealthy about a soul which longs to do any of these things and that the worthy soul has no desire to commit any of these evils and consequently suffers no pain in refraining from doing them.

The Mutakallimun are the groups of Arabic philosophers whose teaching is called the Kalam (an Arabic word meaning speech). Maimonides evidently feels that the Jewish thinkers who use the term "rational precepts" for rules which man can work out for himself without the help of Scripture, have been too much influenced by external ideas. Maimonides himself would prefer to use a term such as "rational precepts" for a different idea, namely that some precepts have to do with the reason, with man's thinking. Later on in the discussion Maimonides quotes a traditional Jewish term which he prefers.

But when the sages say that the man who exercises self-control is superior and that his reward is the greater they are thinking of the traditional religious commands. Of these it is true that were it not for the Torah which has forbidden them they would not be evil at all. Consequently, with regard to these matters they say that a man must allow his soul to love them so that the only motive he will have for rejecting them is obedience to the Torah.

Maimonides' distinction is subtle. Things such as murder and theft are evil in themselves (because someone is harmed by them) and no reasonable person ought to wish to do them. But the sages are speaking of religious laws and with regard to these (even though they no doubt have value in themselves) the chief point is obedience to God. If a man simply had a physical distaste for a mixture of meat and milk there would be no evidence at all of any religious motivation if he refrained from eating it. Furthermore, why should he be considered superior merely because he has a physical distaste for a particular kind of food? This has nothing to do with character except for the element of obedience to God's law, and obedience implies a struggle!

Examine carefully the wise words of the sages and the type of illustration they give. For they do not say: "A man should not say: It is impossible for me to murder. It is impossible for me to steal. It is impossible for me to cheat. But he should say: It is possible, but what can I do if my Father in Heaven has ordered me not to do it." All the illustrations they give are of purely traditional religious matters: meat and milk, mixed garments and forbidden sexual unions. Such precepts are called by God in Scripture "statutes." The Rabbis understand the term to mean "decrees which I have given you and which you must not question." And they say that the heathen argue against them and Satan ridicules them; for example, the law of the red heifer and the scapegoat. As for those precepts which the later thinkers call "rational" the sages call them "precepts" as they have explained the matter.

Satan, for Maimonides, is the name given to something in man which takes delight in ridiculing God's commands. The law of the red heifer is found in Numbers 19 and the law of the scapegoat in Leviticus 16:20-22. These are examples of strange laws which the heathen and Satan roundly declare to be nonsensical. Indeed, they are, says Maimonides in so many words, were it not for the fact that God has so decreed and it is this which endows them with significance. Maimonides refers to the Rabbinic interpretation of the two terms: statutes (ḥukim) and precepts (mitzvot). The first are simply divine decrees which have no reason clear to man but are tests of obedience to God. The precepts (mitzvot) are what the later Jewish thinkers (as Maimonides says, under the influence of the Kalam) call "rational precepts."

It will now be clear to you from all that we have said with regard to which sins the man who does not desire them can be said to be superior to the man who does desire them but controls himself, and with regard to which sins the opposite is true. This is a marvellous and original interpretation. If you place the two sets of sayings side by side and note the language used in each you will see how correct our interpretation is. Our intention in this chapter has now been adequately covered.

Maimonides adds a final support for his distinction. The philosophers, when they discuss this subject, clearly refer to the "rational precepts," while the language used by the sages shows that they refer to the "statutes." Some later Jewish thinkers feel that Maimonides' distinction is a little too neat. We can imagine the case of a man, for instance, severely tempted to steal because of his poverty but who struggles with himself not to do so. In many ways such a person is greater than the man who enjoys a placid existence and never had any temptation to steal.

How the good Jew should behave

How one may develop a well-balanced character.

People physically ill sometimes find bitter things sweet to their taste and sweet things bitter. It even happens that sick people have a longing for things not fit to eat such as dust or charcoal and they hate good food like bread and meat, depending upon how sick they are. The same applies to people whose soul is sick. They desire, even love, holding evil opinions and they hate the good way along which they are too lazy to walk so that, in their sickness, they find it extremely burdensome. Of such people Isaiah says: "Woe unto them that call evil good, and good evil; that change darkness into light, and light into darkness; that change bitter into sweet, and sweet into bitter" (Isaiah 5:20). What should the sick in soul do in order to be cured? They should go to the wise men, the doctors of the soul, who will cure their sickness by teaching them how to behave until they come back to the good way. People who are aware of their bad character but refuse to go to the wise to be cured, of them Solomon says: "The foolish despise wisdom and discipline" (Proverbs 1:7).

Maimonides was a physician of note as well as a great Jewish thinker and teacher. The comparison of physical sickness with spiritual disease would naturally have occurred to him.

What form should their cure take? If a man is hot tempered he is taught to behave in such a way that he does not feel hurt even if he is beaten or reviled. He should behave in this way for so long a period that his quick temper is torn out of his heart. If a man is arrogant he should allow himself to be despised to the extent of sitting beneath everyone else, of wearing rags, which make others despise the wearer, and do things of like nature until the arrogance is torn out of his heart so that he can then return to the middle way, which is the good way. Once he has returned to the middle way he should follow it all the days of his life. He should behave in this way with regard to every other character trait. If he is too far in the direction of one extreme he should go to the opposite extreme for a long period until he comes back to the middle way, namely, the average way in each character trait.

Maimonides, following the teachings of Aristotle on Ethics, is a great believer in the middle way. He argues that extremes of character and disposition are unreasonable. For instance, a man should not be a spendthrift nor should he be a miser but he should adopt the middle way between these extremes. He should not be greedy nor should he be too generous. (Later Jewish thinkers at times criticize Maimonides as being too much influenced by the Greeks in his ideal of the harmonious character. The good Jew, they argue, should be extremely generous and kind.) Here Maimonides says that although the extreme way is generally to be avoided, it is the only way of cure for the time being when a man finds himself at the opposite extreme. The commentators give the illustration of a bent bamboo stick which can only be made straight by bending it in the opposite direction.

There are certain traits of character in which it is forbidden to follow the average way but in which one should go to the opposite extreme. One of these is pride. It is not enough for a man to be humble but he should be exceedingly meek and lowly in spirit. This is why Scripture says of Moses that he was "very meek" (Numbers 12:3) and not simply "meek." This is why the sages command: "Be exceedingly lowly of spirit." Anger, too, is a very bad quality and it is right for man to depart from it to the opposite extreme, training himself never to lose his temper even when he is entitled to do so.

If he wishes to be stern with his children and the members of his family or with the community of which he is the leader, and he wishes to be angry with them in order to improve their conduct, he should appear to them as if he is angry in order to rebuke them but he should be inwardly serene. He should act like one who pretends to be angry but is not really so. The sages of old say that anyone who flies into a rage is like an idolator. And they said further that whoever loses his temper loses his wisdom if he is a sage and if he is prophet his prophetic capacity departs from him. They said further that the lives of those who fly into rages are not worth living. This is why they order a man to be so far from anger as not to feel even those things which are provocative and this is a good way. It is the way of the righteous that they allow themselves to be insulted but they themselves never insult others. They do not reply when they hear others reviling them. They do everything in love and rejoice in this sort of suffering. Of them Scripture says: "But they that love Him be as the sun when he goeth forth in his might" (Judges 5:31).

The middle way does not apply to pride and anger. Man should go to extremes in avoiding these. However, he should not go so far as to abase himself by dressing in rags or sitting beneath other men unless it is to effect the cure Maimonides mentions in the previous paragraph.

A man should always practice silence, never opening his mouth to speak unless it is either with words of wisdom or with talk of those things he needs for his physical well-being. They said of Rav, the pupil of our holy teacher, that he never said anything that was unnecessary in all his life. This refers to the kind of talk most men indulge in. A man should not speak too much even of those matters which concern his physical well-being. Concerning this the sages commanded saying: "Whoever indulges in too much talk brings about sin." And they further said: "I have found nothing better for the body than silence." Even with regard to subjects of Torah and wisdom a man's words should be few in quantity but rich in quality. This is why the sages command: "A man should always teach his pupils in a concise manner." But if the words are rich in quantity but poor in content this is stupidity, concerning which it is said:

"For a dream cometh through a multitude of business; and a fool's voice through a multitude of words" (Ecclesiastes 5:2).

Maimonides' views on silence may strike some people as rather extreme. The holy teacher is Rabbi Judah the Prince, editor of the Mishnah (second century), who is so called in the Rabbinic literature. Rav, his pupil, is the famous Babylonian teacher.

"Silence is a fence to wisdom." A man should not, therefore, be quick to reply to a question and should not say too much. He should teach his pupils quietly and serenely without raising his voice loudly and without using any unnecessary expressions. It is to this that Solomon refers when he says: "The words of the wise are spoken in quiet" (Ecclesiastes 9:17).

Maimonides begins this paragraph with a Rabbinic quote which means that silence helps to preserve wisdom.

It is forbidden for a man to accustom himself to use smooth and deceptive language. He should not say one thing when he means another but his inner thoughts should be in accord with the impression he gives and his mouth should utter that which he really thinks. It is forbidden to mislead anyone, even a heathen. He should not urge someone to be his guest knowing full well that he will not agree to it nor should he try to persuade someone to accept a gift if he knows full well that he will not accept it. Nor should he seek to persuade someone that he has opened a jar of wine in his honor when he has, in fact, opened it for sale. The same applies to all similar matters. Even one word of smooth talk or misrepresentation is forbidden but a man should have true lips, a sincere spirit and a heart free of any trickery and deceit.

A man should neither be frivolous and jesting nor miserable and melancholy, but serene. Our sages say: "Jesting and frivolity accustom a man to lewdness." They ordered a man to be indulgent neither in laughter nor in mourning and sadness but to receive everyone with a cheerful face. So, too, a man should neither be too ambitious and greedy for gain, nor so pessimistic that he never achieves anything. But he should be generous, doing a little business and studying the Torah, and he should rejoice in the little that has fallen to his lot, without being quarrelsome or envious or lustful or avid for fame. The sages say: "Jealousy, lust and ambition put a man out of this world." To sum up: a man should always adopt the average in each trait of character until all his character traits are directed toward the middle way. This is what Solomon means when he says: "Balance the path of thy feet, and let all thy ways be established" (Proverbs 4:26).

CHAPTER 4

NAHMANIDES: LETTER 9, COLLECTED WRITINGS,
ED. C. B. CHAVEL, JERUSALEM, 1963, PAGE 374f

On humility

The root of all the other virtues.

"Hear, my son, the instruction of thy father, and forsake not the teaching of thy mother" (Proverbs 1:8).

Train yourself always to speak softly to every man. You will then avoid anger than which there is no worse trait for it brings a man to sin. Our Rabbis say: "Whoever flies into a rage, every kind of Hell has dominion over him. As it is said: "Therefore remove anger from thy heart, and put away evil from thy flesh" (Ecclesiastes 11:10). "Evil" here means "Hell," as it is said: "Yea, even the wicked for the day of evil" (Proverbs 16:4).

When you are saved from anger your heart will embrace the trait of humility than which nothing is better, as it is said: "The reward of humility is the fear of the Lord" (Proverbs 22:4). As a result of humility the fear of the Lord will enter your heart. For you will reflect upon whence you came and whither you are going, and that even in your lifetime you are a worm and a maggot, how much more so after your death. And you will reflect that you will be called upon to give a full account of your deeds before the King of glory. As it is said: "Behold, heaven and the heaven of heavens cannot contain Thee; how much less the hearts of the children of men!" (I Kings 8:27 and Proverbs 15:11). And it says further: "Do I not fill heaven and earth? saith the Lord" (Jeremiah 23:24). And when

19

you think on all these matters you will fear your Creator and keep yourself from sin. In this way you will always be happy in the portion to which you are entitled. When you conduct yourself in humility, being shy before men, in awe of God and fearful of sin, the Divine Presence and its glory will rest upon you and you will live a life of heavenly bliss even on earth. Know, now, my son, and see that whoever exalts himself over others in his heart rebels against the Kingdom of Heaven for he adorns himself by putting on God's garment, as it is said: "The Lord reigneth; He is clothed with pride" (Psalms 93:1).

Of what can a man be proud in his heart? If it is in his riches, "The Lord maketh poor, and maketh rich" (I Samuel 2:7). If it is in the honor people pay him, behold this is God's, as it is said: "Both riches and honor come of Thee" (I Chronicles 29:12) and how dare he glorify himself with the honor of his Maker? And if he glories in his wisdom then "He removeth the speech of men of trust, and taketh away the sense of the elders" (Job 12:20). It follows that God is indifferent to man's boasting for in His anger He brings the proud low, and if He wills it He exalts the lowly. Therefore be humble and God will lift you up.

I shall, therefore, explain to you how to conduct yourself with humility and how to make this virtue your own at all times. All your words should be spoken gently. Your head should be bent, your eyes gazing downward to the ground and your heart upward. When you address someone do not look him in the face. Let every man seem superior to you in your own eyes. If he is wise or rich you have reason to respect him. If he is poor and you are richer or wiser than he, think to yourself that you are therefore all the more blameworthy and he all the less, for if you sin you do so intentionally whereas he only sins unintentionally.

In whatever you do and whenever you speak or think or, indeed, at all times, imagine yourself standing in the presence of God. For His glory fills all the earth. Let your words be in dread and fear as a slave in his master's presence. And be shy of all men. If anyone calls to you do not answer with a loud voice but gently and in soft voice as one who stands in the presence of a great man.

Be careful always to read the Torah so as to be able to fulfill it. Whenever you rise from reading a book examine what you have studied to see if there is anything you can put into practice. Examine your deeds carefully morning and evening, and so all your days will be spent in repentance.

Remove all worldly cares from your heart at the time of prayer. Prepare your heart before God and purify your thoughts. Before you allow any words to escape your lips think on what you are about to say. If you do this in all matters all the days of your life you will not sin. All your deeds will then be upright and your prayers clear, pure and well-intentioned and they will be acceptable to God. As it is said: "Thou wilt direct their heart, Thou wilt cause Thine ear to attend" (Psalms 10:17).

Read this letter once a week and do not fail to keep its instructions. Let this always be your direction in following after God so that all your ways may prosper. You will then be worthy of all the good that is stored up for the righteous.

This famous letter (it is printed in some editions of the prayerbook) was written by Naḥmanides (Moses ben Naḥman) to his son Naḥman. Note how, after the fashion of those days, the points Naḥmanides makes are supported by quotations from the Bible and Rabbinic literature. Jewish teachers like Naḥmanides did not offer advice on human conduct as if it were their own personal opinion but as the teaching of the Torah. So they gave support to their counsel by citing the classical Jewish sources. This can lead to a problem. The prophets and sages often used metaphors and similes to make their point. They regularly employed a poetic and symbolic way of speaking. Hyperbole, exaggeration in order to make a point, is one of their most common literary devices. Later writers copied their style but sometimes they or their readers took as literal truth what would seem to have originally been poetic figure. So here some might think that humility is praised in too extreme terms. Is it necessary, or even right, for example, that a man should think of himself as a worm or that he should look upon every man as superior to him? Yet Naḥmanides is making reference here to certain Rabbinic statements about man which his son knew very well. Because present day readers do not instantly think of all the Rabbinic maxims which lie behind almost every sentence, they may take Naḥmanides more literally than he intended. The letter remains, however, a noble example of how a truly great man (Naḥmanides was one of the most outstanding scholars of the Middle Ages) valued humility.

CHAPTER 5

On charity

Some of the limits to giving charity.

The community leaders noticed that a good Jew in their town of-
ered hospitality to visitors. He was once a rich man who made guests
so welcome that they constantly visited him. After a time he lost
his wealth but the guests continued to come to him. The members
of the town council were then duty bound to say privately to this
man: "We know that you are unable to spend so much on your
guests, but since they still come to you please take this charity
money so that you can continue to supply them with food and
drink." It is in order for the man to inform his guests that the money
he now supplies them with is charity money so that they should not
imagine that they owe him a personal debt of gratitude for all he
does for them. If, however, the guests think that the money he
spends on them is his own, and if they knew that it was charity
money they would not accept it out of shame, it is better not to
tell them the truth. Even though they will then think that it is his
own money he is spending on them, this is not to be compared to
misrepresentation since he has not misled them, they have misled
themselves. Furthermore even if the host, a poor God-fearing man
who has lost his money, is ashamed to admit to his guests that he is
using charity money, it is no worse than the man who says to the

charity overseers: "Give me charity money for myself" and he gives the money he receives to the poor. Concerning such a case it is said: "Happy is he that considereth the poor" (Psalms 41:2).

Rabbi Judah ben Samuel of Regensburg belonged to the circle known as the Ḥasidé Ashkenaz, The German Saints, at the end of the twelfth century. This was a group of especially pious Jews and the Book of Saints is their textbook. In it a rather naive but very deep kind of piety is expressed. These men tried to live worthily in every part of their lives. Charity, fellow feeling and correct behavior at all times are the ideas especially stressed in this passage.

A man was accustomed to give money to a poor man. He gave him large amounts of money over the years but now the poor man realizes that the once rich man can no longer afford to help him. If the poor man senses that if his benefactor will not give to him he will not give to anyone else either, since he has nothing to give, but might continue to give to him out of embarrassment, then the poor man should refuse to accept his gifts. If the poor man is not sure whether the benefactor can still afford to give to him, he should find out through a third person so as not to embarrass him. So too the charity collectors should not ask for money from someone who cannot afford to give for he may be too embarrassed to refuse to give and they will have committed a sin.

It is wrong for charity collectors to take money from someone who cannot afford to give.

A guest eating in a house in which he has been offered hospitality should leave something on his plate in order to show that he was given more than enough. If he eats everything, people might say that it is because he was not given sufficient. If, however, the host said to him: "Please do not leave anything. What is the good of throwing food to the dogs!" he should obey the host and leave nothing on his plate. Furthermore, if they have to throw away whatever he leaves he will be guilty of the offense of wasting food.

The Rabbis say that it is forbidden to waste food and base this on the verse in Deuteronomy 20:19-20: "Only the trees of which thou knowest that they are not trees for food, them thou mayest destroy and cut down."

It once happened that a certain guest regularly took no notice of his host who urged him to eat well. When the host observed this he naturally gave him smaller portions and then the guest complained. A sage said to the guest: Your host was quite right for you should have listened to him in the first place. Your intention was to pay him honor but the best way of honoring a man is to do what he wants.

A guest should not bring into the home which offers him hospitality another guest. If Reuven gives a gift to Simeon, Simeon should not say to Reuven: Give something also to Levi for my sake. However, he may do so if Reuven said to Simeon: Please tell me who else is in need that I might help him.

Reuven said to Simeon: I can only afford to support one poor person and not two. If you want I shall support you, and he supported Simeon. Simeon then went and told Levi. Levi came to Reuven and said: Support me. Reuven replied: I am sorry I cannot do that because I am supporting Simeon. Simeon begged Reuven to support Levi as well. Reuven thereupon gave up supporting Simeon and began to support Levi instead. Simeon complained: Why have you stopped supporting me? Reuven replied: You bothered me so much that I substituted Levi for you. You had no pity on me when I told you that I could not afford to support Levi as well and could only support one person and yet you kept at me. All I could do was to support him instead of you. In connection with such a case it is said: "He that blesseth his friend with a loud voice, rising early in the morning, it shall be counted a curse to him" (Proverbs 27:14).

"And it was so, that when he had turned his back to go from Samuel, God gave him another heart" (I Samuel 10:9). From this it appears that Samuel stood up and Saul asked permission to take leave of him.

When a man accompanies his friend about to leave on a journey the traveler should ask his friend for leave before turning to go on his journey and his friend should remain standing in his place. If a man about to embark on a journey senses that it is bothersome for his friend to accompany him part of the way, he should beg him to remain where he is and the friend should then remain standing while he takes his departure. As it is said: "And the men turned from thence . . . but Abraham stood yet before the Lord" (Genesis 18:22). And it is further said: "When he turned his back to go from Samuel, God gave him there another heart" (I Samuel 10:9). "There" means not in the presence of Samuel, so as not to suggest that Samuel was responsible for his new heart. For later on, when Saul went to Samuel to seek David at Naioth (I Samuel 19:18-24), he prophesied when he turned his back that he, Samuel, had nothing to do with Saul's new heart which urged him to wage war. This capacity was rather given to Saul by the power of the oil with which he was anointed king and was not due at all to Samuel. "The king's heart is in the hand of the Lord as the watercourses: He turneth it whithersoever He will" (Proverbs 21:1). If king and people deserve it God turns the king's heart for good and it is accounted to the king for righteousness. But if people and king do not deserve it, God turns the king's heart for evil and the king is then punished for not being deserving enough to have his heart turned for good.

Whoever gives charity to the poor for the sake of Heaven God sows it like seed for him. That is to say, if he gives some money or something of value or gives some pleasure to a poor man—all in proportion to wealth and poverty, since a small amount given by a poor man is equal to a large amount given by a rich man—God sows it in Paradise where it grows year by year. The produce thereof is stored up for him in a storehouse together with all kinds of precious fruits which he will enjoy in the World to Come. As it is said: "For as the earth bringeth forth her growth, and as the garden causeth the things that are sown in it to spring forth; so the Lord God will cause charity to spring forth" (Isaiah 61:11). And it is written: "Light is sown for the righteous" (Psalms 97:11). And it is written: "At our doors are all manner of precious fruits" (Song of Songs 7:14). And it is written: "Is not this laid up in store with Me, sealed up in My treasuries?" (Deuteronomy 32:34). And it is written: "Sow to yourselves according to righteousness, reap according to mercy" (Hosea 10:12). For whoever gives pleasure to others his righteousness is assessed according to the pleasure and the deed. If a poor man gives a small coin to another poor man it is better than when a rich man gives many coins.

The point about Samuel and Saul is none too clear but seems to be that Saul wished to believe that the oil with which he was anointed king was what gave him power, not Samuel's blessing, and, therefore, Samuel had no right to take the power from him.

On speaking evil

How we may know when our talk about others is sinful.

There are six types of evil talkers. The first is the man who finds faults with others when they have no faults and sometimes blames those who are not only innocent of the fault but are worthy people. Such a person embraces both the evils of falsehood and slander. The Torah warns us not to listen to slander because it might be false and a lie, as it is said: "Thou shalt not utter a false report" (Exodus 23:1).

You should know that whoever agrees with a slanderous statement when he hears it is as bad as the one who utters it for everyone will say that the report must be true since those who heard it agreed with it. Even if the hearer only turns to listen to the slanderous report and gives the impression of believing it to be true he helps the evil, brings disgrace upon his neighbor and encourages slanderers to bring their evil reports to peoples' ears.

The second type is the man who speaks evil of others but is careful not to say anything that is untrue. The Rabbis speak of this when they say that there is not only a class of liars but also a separate class of people who offer evil reports (even if they do not tell lies).

Now if a man reminds his neighbor in private of the evil deeds done by the latter's ancestors he offends against the law in the Torah: "Ye shall not wrong one another" (Leviticus 25:17), which deals with "wronging with words," as we have earlier explained. The Torah specifically says: "The son shall not bear the iniquity of the father" (Ezekiel 18:20). If one shames another in public because of his ancestors' deeds our Rabbis say that whoever puts his neighbor to shame in public will go to Hell and not emerge from there. Even if he tells others, when his neighbor is not present, about the abominations done by the latter's ancestors in order to destroy his reputation and bring disgrace upon him, of such an evil-talker the Rabbis say that he is a member of the class of those who offer evil reports and he will not see the Divine Presence. The same applies to anyone who tells others about the former behavior of a sinner who has repented.

You should know that if a man sees his neighbor offending against the Torah in secret and he tells what he saw publicly he is to be blamed for this. For it is possible that the sinner has turned away from his evil way and is now sorry for what he has done and bitter at heart. It is wrong, therefore, to reveal it except to a discreet and wise man who will not tell others about it but will simply avoid the sinner's company until he is sure that he has repented. If, however, the sinner is a scholar and a God-fearing man it is right to take it for granted that he has truly repented and that although his evil inclination got the better of him once, now his soul is bitter at his own failing.

Whoever repeats evil things about others does two evils. First he causes harm to others and brings disgrace upon them. Secondly, he demonstrates that he is pleased to be able to blame others and to rejoice in their downfall. From one point of view it is worse to repeat an evil report that is true than to repeat one that is false. The public is more likely to believe things that are true. Thus the reputation of the one spoken about will be damaged and he will be treated with disdain, even though he has repented and been pardoned for his sin.

You should know, however, that in matters where the happiness of other human beings is at stake, for instance, in cases of theft, oppression, assault, causing others pain or putting them to shame, or wronging others, it is permitted for the person who witnessed the offense to repeat it to others in order to help the victim and be zealous for truth. The Torah rules that a single witness should testify in court where there is a monetary claim in order to compel the defendant to take an oath. However, in such cases he should first rebuke the offender.

The third type is the talebearer. We have been warned against this in the Torah: "Thou shalt not go up and down as a talebearer among thy people" (Leviticus 19:16). There are no limits to the harm done by the talebearer for he adds to hatred in the world and causes others to offend against the command of the Torah which reads: "Thou shalt not hate thy brother in thy heart" (Leviticus 19:17). We have explained earlier that the world can only endure if there is peace but where there is hatred the earth and all its inhabitants totter. It frequently happens that the talebearer places a sword in the hands of the one to whom he tells it in order to slay his neighbor, as it is said: "In thee have been talebearers to shed blood" (Ezekiel 22:9). Greater than any other offense of evil talk is when one stirs up trouble between brothers and friends, causing them to hate one another, as it is said: "And he that soweth discord among brethren" (Proverbs 6:19). The Rabbis say that this is the seventh offense mentioned in these verses and is the worst of them all.

A man is duty bound to keep any secret his neighbor has imparted to him even though no talebearing is involved if the secret is revealed. For to tell another's secret is to harm him and frustrate his plans. Secondly, anyone who reveals a secret acts in an immodest manner and offends against his neighbor who begged him to keep it secret.

The fourth type is the *dust* of evil talk. Our Rabbis say that all men are guilty of the *dust* of evil talk. They used the term for a man who speaks words which bring others to speak evil. They said, for instance, that a man should not speak well of his neighbor for this may result in others speaking evil of him. Now this needs to be understood for it is well known how good it is to praise wise and good men and one definition the Rabbis give of an ignoble man is that he never speaks well of others. The answer is as follows. One should only speak well of a man in private, that is to say from person to person, and not in public unless it is known that of all the people present there is none who hates the man spoken of and none who envies him. If, however, one wishes to praise a man with a universal reputation for goodness and without blame or guilt it is proper to praise him even in the presence of his enemies or of those jealous of him for if any of them begins to speak evil of him all will know that he lies and is only putting himself in the wrong.

Another example is given by the Rabbis. Suppose a woman asks her neighbor for fire from her hearth and she replies: Where is fire to be found if not in the house of so-and-so where they are always roasting meat to eat? In any such remarks one has committed the offense of the *dust* of evil talk. It is said: "He that blesseth his friend with a loud voice, rising early in the morning, it shall be counted a curse to him" (Proverbs 27:14). The Rabbis apply this verse to one who praises his neighbor in such a way as to cause him harm. For instance, a guest who goes out into the street and shouts aloud how good his host has been to him so that unworthy people hear of it and force themselves on the host. A man is obliged to take care that when he speaks no one will suspect him of having the intention of speaking evil, for if he becomes suspect in this way he has acted unethically and is guilty of the *dust* of evil talk.

The fifth type is unclean talk.

The sixth type is the complainer. The complainer is the man who is always grumbling and whining and finding fault with his friend's conduct and speech even though the friend is quite innocent of any desire to harm him. Such a person always finds reasons for accusing, never for excusing. He treats every unintentional slight as if it were intentional. He imagines himself to be victimized and is full of his neighbor's sins against him whereas in reality he is the offender. It often happens that the complainer is ungrateful. He imagines that harm has been done to him even when, in fact, good has been done and he repays good with evil. Sometimes he even goes so far as to imagine that God's kindnesses are punishments and retribution. Keep yourself, therefore, far from the way of the complainers for they harm only themselves and know not of peace. Teach your tongue to find excuses for others and let your loins be girded with righteousness.

This lengthy passage in the original text has been slightly abbreviated to make for easier reading. Note the skillful way in which Rabbi Jonah quotes Scriptural verses to make his points. There is, of course, an element of hyperbole in some of the sayings as when he speaks of Hell. Rabbi Jonah was numbered among the opponents of Maimonides but when he saw the harm caused by the controversy and the wicked things people had said of the great teacher he was big enough to change his mind and feel sorry for the part he had played in the affair. It is rumored that he wrote this book in an effort to repent, which would explain the harsh things he has to say about evil talk. He remarks that there are six types of evil talk: 1) False and evil talk about others; 2) True but evil talk about others; 3) Talebearing; 4) The dust of evil talk i.e. talk which is not evil in itself but can lead to it; 5) Dirty talk; 6) Ungrateful and complaining talk, having a chip on one's shoulder. Pious Jews used to read the Gates of Repentance during the Ten Days of Penitence from Rosh Hashanah to Yom Kippur.

CHAPTER 7

ISAAC ABOAB: MENORAT HA-MAOR, "CANDELABRA OF LIGHT," II, 2:2

On truth and falsehood

The boundary between white lies and ordinary lies.

We must know that the world exists because of truth, as we have been taught in the first chapter of *Ethics of the Fathers:* **Rabban Simeon ben Gamaliel said: The world depends for its existence on three things: on justice, on truth and on peace. It is obvious that there is no need for justice where there is peace and peace is found where there is truth. All three are therefore embraced by truth and this is why it is placed between the others in the saying. The world was created with truth alone. This is why truth is referred to by hint at the beginning of the creation story (Genesis 1:1) in the final letters of bereshit bara elohim and also at the end of the section (Genesis 2:3) bara elohim laasot. This is to teach us that everything brought into being during the six days of creation depends for its continued existence upon truth. God's name is truth, as it is said: "The Lord God is truth" (Jeremiah 10:10) and the Torah is called truth, as it is said: "And Thy Torah is truth" (Psalms 119:142).**

The Candelabra of Light *is Rabbi Isaac Aboab's collection of Rabbinic sayings with lengthy comments of his own. It is a kind of encyclopedia of Jewish ethics. The work is divided into seven main parts (corresponding to the seven branches of the Temple candelabra) and sub-divided into smaller sections and sub-sections. This passage has been slightly abbreviated to avoid some difficult*

*punning and word-play which cannot be adequately conveyed
in English. An example here is Rabbi Aboab's statement that
the Hebrew word for truth is hinted at in the creation story. "In
the beginning God . . ." is, in Hebrew, bereshit bara elohim. The
final letters of these words are: tav, alef, mem, and these are also
the final letters of the last three Hebrew words in the creation story.
These three letters are the letters of the Hebrew word for truth,
emet. Rabbi Aboab calls this a hint.*

**Even comparatively harmless lies are forbidden. There are people,
for example, who tell lies whenever they relate events which happened without any gain to themselves and without causing harm to
others but they imagine that the telling of untruths is of some benefit
to them and the relating of things otherwise than they really are.
This, too, is forbidden on the grounds of "They have taught their
tongue to speak lies, they weary themselves to commit iniquity"
(Jeremiah 9:4) even though the penalty for this is less severe than
the penalty to those who tell lies in order to mislead others or to
harm them.**

**Our Rabbis went further to say that every God-fearing person should
keep a promise even if he only made it in his heart, as we find in
the story of Rav Safra to whom the verse was applied: "And speaketh
truth in his heart" (Psalms 15:2).**

*The story of Rav Safra is told in the Talmud. He was approached
to sell something he had and was offered a price which suited him
but he was unable at the time to signify his consent because
he was reciting his prayers and was unable to interrupt. The
buyer, seeing that Rav Safra had apparently disregarded his bid,
kept on increasing the price but Rav Safra insisted on selling
it for the original price which the buyer had offered and to
which he had agreed "in his heart."*

**However, if it is for the sake of peace it is permitted to lie. As the
Rabbis say: It is permitted to tell lies for the sake of promoting
peace. They say that it is permitted to praise a bride in the presence
of her groom by saying that she is beautiful and kind even if she**

is not so that her husband will be pleased with her. In spite of this a man should not accustom himself to tell lies even about inconsequential matters in order not to train his tongue to speak falsely. As the Rabbis say: Rav was constantly tormented by his wife. If he told her to prepare lentils she would prepare small peas and if he asked for small peas she would prepare lentils. When his son Ḥiyya grew up he gave her his father's instructions in the reverse order. Rav said to him: Your mother has improved. Ḥiyya replied: It was I who reversed your instructions to her. Rav said: Now I understand the popular saying: Your children teach you to behave reasonably. Nevertheless do not do this any longer, for it is said: "They have taught their tongue to speak lies" (Jeremiah 9:4). A man should consequently train his tongue to speak the truth and the God of truth will lead him in the way of truth.

A white lie is permitted. The reason it is wrong to lie is because of the harm it may cause, but when it is in order to promote peace it does good and not harm and is consequently permitted.

There are other matters which fall under the heading of falsehood; for example, when a man praises himself for having virtues he does not really possess. It sometimes happens that a man may persuade his friend into believing that he has spoken well of him or done him a good turn when, in fact, he has done nothing of the kind. In this connection our Rabbis teach that it is forbidden to mislead others even if they are heathens. Another example is one who promises to do something for his neighbor and fails to carry out his promise. All this is to fulfill the verse: "The remnant of Israel shall not do iniquity, nor speak lies, neither shall a deceitful tongue be found in their mouth" (Zephaniah 3:13). The meaning is that even where nothing iniquitous is involved they shall not have a deceitful tongue in their mouths but all their words should be truthful.

Some liars mislead their neighbors into believing that they are friends and have their welfare at heart, but their real purpose is only to win their neighbor's confidence so as to be able to harm him. Of them it is said: "One speaketh peaceably to his neighbor with his mouth, but in his heart he layeth wait for him" (Jeremiah 9:7).

The verse goes on to say: "Shall I not punish them for these things? saith the Lord; shall not My soul be avenged on such a nation as this?" (Jeremiah 9:8). Other liars have their eyes on future benefits and tell lies in order to persuade their neighbors to give them gifts. Other liars mislead their neighbors by telling lies so as to obtain something of value from them or from others so that they can steal it for themselves. The Rabbis compare this to idolatry for this is precisely what the idolators do when they pretend that their gods have power.

Worse than any of these are those who cheat with false weights and measures or deny that they owe a debt when in reality they do, or deny that something has been deposited with them when in fact it has. Such persons are called scoundrels because they are guilty of falsehood, robbery and covetousness. Regarding them Scripture says: "Ye shall not steal; neither shall ye deal falsely, nor lie to one another" (Leviticus 19:11). Not content with this they bring about quarrels and strife, murder and false oaths and many other sins.

All these evils result when a man accustoms himself to speak falsehood and when he takes pride in so doing. For it may cause him to shed the innocent blood of the victim if he challenges him, either directly or by informing against him, or he will plan evil for him and run to do him every kind of evil. And if he cannot do him harm in any other way, he will give false testimony against him in order to destroy him. And if he is unable to testify against him he will become a talebearer to stir up mischief even between brothers. So all these evils can result from falsehood. Therefore Scripture says: "Keep thee far from a false matter" (Exodus 23:7) and it goes on to say: "and the innocent and the righteous slay thou not" to teach us that falsehood can lead to the murder of innocent people.

Happy, therefore, is the man who keeps himself far from falsehood and trains his mouth to speak truth and righteousness. If he follows in this way he will attain all his wishes in this world and the next, he will train his children in the way of righteousness and he will be saved from all trouble.

Aboab's conclusion that the man who speaks the truth will "attain all his wishes" and be "saved from all trouble" is not, of course, a real guarantee. Honest people sometimes fail to succeed but since they are fundamentally honest they will remain so even when unsuccessful. Remember that Aboab, like the other writers in this genre, is using hyperbole. Honesty is the best policy even on grounds of pure expediency, but this should not be the motive for the honest life. What Aboab appears to be saying here is that the truthful person has God on his side because God loves men of truth.

CHAPTER 8

On hatred, revenge and pride

Proper and improper love of self.

Man's perverse heart finds it difficult to avoid hatred and revenge. When a man has been insulted, he feels it very strongly and suffers a great deal so that revenge is sweeter to him than honey and he cannot find rest until he gets it. Consequently, if he is brave enough to give up that which his nature compels him to do; if he can forgive the one who has stirred up his hatred and not hate in return; if he takes no revenge even when he has the opportunity of doing so and bears no grudge but forgets it all as if it had not happened, he is, indeed, courageous and heroic. This thing is easy only for the angels who possess no evil traits of character not for "those that dwell in houses of clay, whose foundation is in the dust" (Job 4:19). Yet the King has so decreed and what the Scriptural verses clearly express requires no further elaboration: "Thou shalt not hate thy brother in thy heart. Thou shalt not take vengeance nor bear any grudge against the children of thy people" (Leviticus 19:17-18).

The difference between taking revenge and bearing a grudge is well known. Taking revenge means to refuse to do good to one who had earlier refused to do good to oneself or who had done one positive harm. Bearing a grudge is to do good to someone who has harmed one but to remind him of the wrong he has done. Man's evil inclination always wishes to keep the heart on the boil and seeks always to leave some impression or some reminder of any wrong done to us. Even if it cannot succeed in keeping the matter vividly in recall it seeks to do so in some small way. For example, the evil inclination says to man: Even if you want to give that man that which he refused to give to you when you were in need, at least do not give it to him graciously. Or, if you do not want to harm him there is no need for you to do him a great favor or to give him much help. Or, even if you want to help him a great deal there is no need for you to do it in his presence. Or, there is no need for you to be as friendly with him as before and to be his companion. It is enough if you have so far forgiven him that you do not appear as his enemy. And even if you want to be his friend there is no need for you to show him as much love as before. By means of these and similar smart observations the evil inclination seeks to trap man. Therefore the Torah lays down a general rule which embraces everything. "Thou shalt love thy neighbor as thyself" (Leviticus 19:18). "As thyself" without distinction; "as thyself" without any difference, without trickery and without scheming; literally "as thyself."

Pride means that a man thinks highly of himself and imagines that he deserves to be praised. There may be a number of reasons for him so thinking. One man thinks he is intelligent, another that he is handsome, another that he has dignity, another that he is a great man, another that he is wise. The general principle is this. Whenever a man imagines that he has any of the virtues he is in immediate danger of falling into the trap of pride. However, once a man thinks highly of himself and that he deserves praise the consequences are not one but many, even contradictory, but they all go back to the same cause and all have the same intention.

There is the proud man who thinks to himself that since he is worthy of praise and is, in his own esteem, unique and outstanding, it is proper for him to behave in a special way and conduct himself with great dignity when he walks, when he sits or stands, when he opens his mouth and in whatever he does. He walks slowly and leisurely, step by step. He sits upright. He rises gradually as the snake raises its head. He refuses to converse with just anybody but only with the gentry and even then he will only utter a few words as if an oracle were speaking. He will be pompous in all that he does, in his movements, his eating and drinking, his dressing and in all his ways, as if his flesh were lead and his bones stone or sand.

Another proud man imagines that since he is worthy of praise and has so many good qualities it is necessary for him to make the whole earth tremble at his presence and be terrified of him. It seems not right to him that other men should dare to speak to him or ask him anything. If they do venture to approach him his voice will terrify them and he will confuse them by replying arrogantly, his face wearing a perpetual frown.

Another proud man imagines himself to be so great and so full of dignity that he thinks it quite impossible for him to lose the respect of others and he thinks that he does not need it. To demonstrate that this is so he will behave as a humble person and will display extreme signs of infinite humility. But deep down inside him his heart is puffed up with pride saying: I am so elevated and so full of dignity that I need no outward tokens of respect. I have so much of it that all I can do is to give it up.

Another proud man wants to be so singled out for his virtues and so distinguished in his conduct that it is not enough for him that everyone should praise him for all the other virtues he imagines he possesses but he wants them to praise him, too, for his humility, that he is the most modest of men. This man takes pride in his humility and seeks fame by appearing to run away from it. Such a man will be ready to place himself below people who are really inferior to him and even below the most unworthy because he imagines that in so doing he demonstrates how perfectly humble he really is. He will not accept any titles and refuses all promotion while his heart says to him: In all the earth there is none wiser and more humble than I. However, even though such proud persons appear to succeed in their pretense of humility they cannot avoid circumstances when unwittingly their pride is uncovered like a flame which comes out of a heap of rubbish. Our Rabbis compared such a man to a house full of straw. The house has many holes and when gradually the straw begins to come out at the holes everyone sees that the house is full of straw. So it is with men of this type. They cannot successfully keep secret their true character and their deeds show the kind of people they are so that it can be seen how spurious is their humility and how much pretense there is in their meekness.

Finally there are other proud men whose pride is kept hidden within themselves so that it never shows. But in their hearts they imagine that they are already very wise and know the truth about everything and that few can be so clever. They consequently have no regard for any opinions other than their own, thinking to themselves that anything they find difficult cannot possibly be easy for others. Whatever their mind shows them is so obvious to them and so simple that they take no notice of those who disagree with them, whether they are early authorities or more recent ones, and they have no doubts about the correctness of their opinions.

All these are examples of the results of pride which sets back the wise and makes them foolish. Pride distracts the wisest of men, how much more young pupils who have not served their apprenticeship properly. These latter imagine that the greatest sages are their equals even though they have only just begun to open their eyes. Regarding all these types of pride Scripture says: "Everyone that is proud in his heart is an abomination to the Lord" (Proverbs 16:5). Anyone who wants to acquire the quality of cleanness must cleanse himself of all of these. One should appreciate that pride is nothing more than a form of blindness in which a man cannot see his faults and admit his inferiority. For if he were able to see and to recognize the truth he would depart as far as he could from these crooked and perverse ways.

M. H. Luzzatto's Mesillat Yesharim, "Path of the Upright," is one of the most popular Jewish ethical works. The book is in the form of a commentary to a Talmudic passage in which the second century teacher, Rabbi Phineas ben Yair, gives the different stages on which a man can proceed to the living of a holy life, hence "Path of the Upright." The passage is worth quoting in full: "The knowledge of the Torah leads to watchfulness, watchfulness to zeal, zeal to cleanness, cleanness to abstinence, abstinence to purity, purity to saintliness, saintliness to humility, humility to the fear of sin, and the fear of sin to holiness." This section is from Luzzatto's description of cleanness, which he understands to mean both a purification of deeds and a cleansing of character.

CHAPTER 9

On saintliness

What we should do if we want to be
more than simply good.

The saintly only does good to others, never harm. This applies to their persons, their property and their feelings. With regard to their persons, this means that the saintly one helps others to the utmost of his capacity and tries to spare them from matters that are burdensome to them. This is what the Rabbis mean when they talk of "bearing the yoke of one's neighbor." If his neighbor is in danger of bodily harm and the saintly one is able to prevent it, he should do all he possibly can in this direction. With regard to property, a saintly man should help his neighbor to the best of his means from suffering any loss. It goes without saying that he should avoid causing any damage himself to the property of others, whether private or public. He should remove every potential cause of damage even if at the moment it is unlikely to be harmful. Our Rabbis say: Let your neighbor's property be as dear to you as your own. With regard to feelings, this means that a saintly person should do everything possible to please others by showing them respect and in every other way. It belongs to the quality of saintliness to do anything that brings pleasure into other peoples' lives. It goes without saying that the saintly will do his utmost to avoid causing anyone pain. This is embraced by the principle of lovingkindness. The Rabbis said much in praise of this virtue and of the importance of our obligation to follow it. Included in it is the duty of pursuing peace which is the general way of promoting the happiness of others. I shall now prove all this by referring you to the teachings of our Rabbis even though these matters are really so obvious that no proof is required.

The Talmud tells us that the pupils of R. Zakkai once asked what merit he had that he lived so long. He replied: I never called my neighbor by his nickname and never failed to recite the *Kiddush* over wine on the Sabbath. I had an elderly mother and once she sold her hood in order to provide me with wine for the *Kiddush*. This is an example of saintliness with regard to religious obligations. In reality, since he was so poor that he would not have had wine for the *Kiddush* unless his mother sold her hood, the law exempts him from reciting *Kiddush* over wine. But although the law exempted him he still carried out the precept because he was saintly. And he had so much respect for his neighbor that he refused to call him even by an underogatory nickname, as the commentators to the passage point out. Of Rav Huna we are similarly told that he wore a waistband of straw over his garments because he had sold his waistband in order to buy wine for the *Kiddush*.

We are told in the same passage that when Rabbi Eleazar ben Shammua was asked by his disciples what merit he had that he had lived so long, he replied: "I never used the Synagogue as a shortcut and I never stepped on the heads of the holy people." These are examples of how the saintly shows respect for the Synagogue and for others, by not walking close by while they sit on the ground for this would be disrespectful to them.

Further in the same passage we are told that when R. Pereda was asked what merit he had that had lived so long, he replied: "No one ever reached the house of learning before me, I never recited grace after meals when a descendant of a priestly family was present (but gave him the honor), and I never ate from an animal before the priest's portions were given to him." When R. Nehunya was asked the same question, he replied: "I never gained any honor at the expense of a friend's disgrace and I never went to bed cursing my neighbor (but if I offended I always asked his pardon)." The first part of his saying is illustrated in the passage by a reference to R. Huna who was carrying a spade on his shoulder. R. Ḥanina ben Ḥanilai met R. Huna and wanted to carry the spade for him whereupon R. Huna said: "If you are accustomed to carry a spade in your own town I will let you carry my spade here but if not I do not wish to acquire honor at the expense of your dishonor." The direct meaning of "gaining honor at the expense of a friend's disgrace" is that one should not try to disgrace one's neighbor in order to increase one's own reputation. But for the saintly it is not even right to accept a token of honor given willingly by a neighbor if as a result the neighbor suffers disgrace in some small way.

Similarly, we are told that when R. Zéra was asked the question, he replied: "I have never behaved in a tyrannical fashion in my home; I have never walked in front of a man greater than I; I have never had thoughts of Torah in unclean places; I have never walked four cubits without studying the Torah and wearing *Tefillin;* I have never slept in the House of Study, not even taken a nap there; I have never rejoiced at my neighbor's downfall; and I have never called my neighbor by his nickname." These are examples of the ways of saintliness to which we have referred.

This passage, largely self-explanatory, is from a later section of Luzzatto's work in which he describes what is involved in leading a saintly life. The saintly—the ḥasid—does far more than the law requires of him in his love for God and man.

He could never be satisfied with merely doing the ethical. He is a man who feels one must go beyond its demands. Moreover, he could not separate doing good to his fellow from being right with his God. The familiar categories, ethical and religious, are both too small for him. Rather by bringing them together and raising them to a higher level through the integrity of his life he sets the standard for lesser men to follow.

A letter on ethical conduct

When ethical ideas become truly effective.

I want to tell your honor a new idea I have just thought of. This concerns the meaning of a Rabbinic passage which puzzled me for years. Now I understand it but have told no one else of it. Your honor is the first.

It is well known that the Rabbis say in the Talmud: "In every generation a man is obliged to see himself as if he himself had gone forth out of Egypt." I always found this hard to understand. How is it possible for anyone to obey this rule? They state it as an *obligation* and whenever this term is used it means that there is a real duty. But how is it possible for a man to obey this rule and see himself as if he personally had gone forth out of Egypt? According to my humble mind the thing is quite impossible. I fail to understand how a man can possibly think of himself as having actually gone forth out of Egypt. Even if a rare great man can bring himself to think in this way, how can it be a rule laid down for everyone? Surely not everyone can be so wise. I have given many explanations in former times but they afforded me no real satisfaction. This year, however, with God's help, I hit upon a simple and marvelous explanation to which I attach the greatest significance. Now it is my practice to value the words of the Rabbis so that I do not impart matters of this sort except to someone who can benefit from it. Otherwise it seems to me as if I had literally taken a very valuable object and given it to someone who will throw it away. This is my procedure and I later found in the writings of the sages of old that this is, in fact, how one should behave. Actually this is part of the meaning of the Rabbinic saying: "If you see a generation which loves the Torah spread the Torah abroad. Otherwise keep it to yourself."

How pleasant in this connection is the old maxim quoted by a number of later scholars. It says of wisdom: "Keep it as the generous keep their wealth." This is how I understand the maxim. The generous person sees value in wealth. As the Rabbis say: "The righteous love their money more than themselves. Why? Because they earn it honestly and never steal." This shows that it is right to set a proper value on wealth. Only the person who values money but disregards the value he sets on it when he has to give it away for a good cause or when he is tempted to get it dishonestly is rightly called generous. If, however, a man gives away his money because he does not value it there is no evidence from the gift that he is generous. It should be exactly the same with regard to wisdom. Whoever squanders his learning to all and sundry demonstrates that learning has no value for him, is cheap and deserves no protection. On the other hand the person who is only prepared to share his learning with the wise who can understand it, demonstrates that he is a generous man who wishes to benefit with his learning those capable of appreciating it. This is the meaning of the maxim: "Keep it as the generous keep their wealth." That is to say, just as the truly generous only give the money they value to those who are in need of it, so too only share your learning with those who can appreciate it. You see, I arrived at this idea by my own reasoning but I was glad to find that I had been anticipated by the earlier teachers. Now I know that your honor loves words of Torah and rejoices when he hears them so that I am glad God has given me the opportunity of sharing my thoughts with such a worthy man upon whom they are bound to leave a powerful impression.

In order to explain the saying that a man is obliged to see himself as if he himself had gone forth out of Egypt, I must first explain another Rabbinic saying also dealing with the redemption theme. The Rabbis say that when Ahasuerus gave his ring to Haman to destroy the Jews (Esther 3:10) this had a greater effect on them than all the warnings of the forty-five male prophets and the seven female prophets. All the warnings of the prophets did not have the effect of bringing the Jewish people back to the good way whereas the removal of the king's ring did have this effect. This saying cries out for exposition. What is it trying to tell us? It seems to me that an important and novel idea is mentioned here.

We learn from this saying that even the wisest of men (like the Israelites at the time of the prophets) is not so much impressed with a truth he grasps merely in his head as with a truth he experiences in a personal way (as the Israelites did in the days of Mordecai and Esther). Since the impression of a truth experienced is so much more powerful it is essential for man, so far as he possibly can, to bring theories regarding reward for doing good and punishment for doing evil closer to his experience. That is to say, he should imagine that the sufferings for sin had actually come upon him, God forbid, so that he experiences how hard to bear they really are. As it is said: "It is better to go to the house of mourning, than to go to the house of feasting; . . . and the living will lay it to his heart" (Ecclesiastes 7:2). This means that a man should imagine his own death, not that of someone else. The Rabbis say that a man should remind himself of the day of his death. Why do they say "the day of *his* death"? Obviously it is *his* death that is referred to. But they wish to call attention to the fact that if a man simply thinks of death in the abstract he thinks of the death of others, not his own. Therefore they say "*his* death," stressing that he should depict to himself his own death. And with regard to every other kind of suffering he should imagine it happening to him if he disobeys the Torah. This will be of great help to him in avoiding sin. This, too, is the meaning of the passage about the removal of the king's ring, to teach us that we are obliged to connect the punishment for sin with our own experience. So, too, we find in the book of Exodus: "If thou lend money to any of My people, even to the poor *with thee*" (Exodus

22:24). *Rashi* explains this to mean: Imagine yourself in the poor man's shoes. It is clear what he means. Scripture gives a man advice on how to avoid hard-heartedness to the poor. Imagine yourself in the poor man's shoes. How would you like it if someone refused to lend you money in your need? We see, clearly, that Scripture commands us to bring these matters closer to our own experience.

The main purpose of the festival of Passover and the duty of reminding ourselves of the Exodus is to bring home to us that God is in control of His world. Therefore He punished the Egyptians for their arrogant hearts and saved His people Israel because they turned to Him and kept His charge and cried out to Him. Now it is impossible for anyone to be moved by events which happened long before his day. Consequently, the Rabbis advise us, as we have said, to bring the matter home by bringing it into our own experience. A man should imagine himself to be a slave who has been set free. What would the thoughts of such a man be? He would think on the greatness of his Master who set him free, and would deliver himself and all he possesses to the Master of the Universe. In this way the Exodus will make a powerful impression upon him. It follows that the Rabbis do not mean literally that a man should see himself as if he personally had gone forth out of Egypt for this is only possible for the very wise. Their rule for every man is that he should bring the miracle of the Exodus closer to his experience by imagining that a *similar* event happened to him personally. This is the same type of counsel as contained in the verse: "the poor *with thee*." In this way the miracle will move him. He will see that the world has a Guide; Him will he fear and Him will he serve. And it will be for our good. Selah. The two sayings regarding the Passover redemption and the Purim redemption can now be seen to be complementary.

Please read this slowly and carefully and I trust that you will derive pleasure from it. I anticipate your thanks because my remarks are very important. From the time I had the privilege of enjoying the great light provided by the light of the world, my master and teacher of blessed memory (R. Israel Salanter), and I began to understand a little of the science of ethics *(musar)*, that only this science (together with the wisdom of the Torah which lies in a corner for all to take) can teach a man how to wage the warfare of the Torah, namely the war of man against his own nature, against the brutishness with which man is born. It is a great battle to bring such a tremendous force as human nature under the sway of reason. The warriors are few and are becoming fewer all the time while brute nature increases in power. In addition to the courage a man needs if he is to conquer his own nature, he needs to recognize the many cunning ways by which the evil inclination seeks to mislead men and to trap them. All this is embraced by the science of ethics (musar).

Rabbi Simḥah Züssel of Kelm was the main disciple of Rabbi Israel Salanter, the founder of the Musar movement in nineteenth century Lithuania. The main aim of the Movement, as this lengthy passage seeks to demonstrate, is to make the traditional ethical teachings of Judaism something more than mere theory by bringing them home to man in his personal life. The followers of the Movement engaged in acute psychological investigations into human nature with the aim of refining man's character and redeeming it from crudeness and brutality. On the whole the Movement had a very somber approach to life (see the references to death and punishment in this letter) and on these grounds and others had its severe critics.

Many today question, and rightly so, whether the fear of punishment is a proper motive for doing good and refraining from evil and whether, indeed, such fear is psychologically wholesome. Some might also be bothered by R. Simḥah Züssel's enthusiasm for his own ideas which would seem to conflict with Jewish teachings on the value of humility. But it can be argued that a truly humble person thinks little of himself and much of the truth so that he is ready to sing the praises of a true idea even if he himself is its author. He tends to think of the idea as coming to him as a gift of God not through any merit of his own. It might also be mentioned that the mood expressed here by R. Simḥah Züssel is akin to what is known nowadays as existentialism. The existentialist approach urges us to see ideas not in the abstract but in vivid relation to our personal lives.

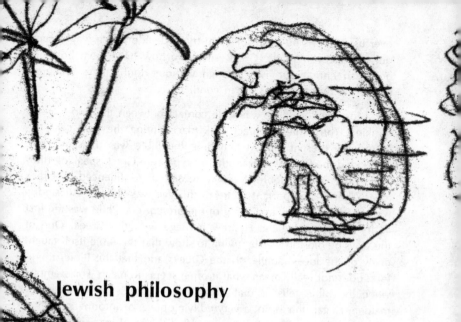

Jewish philosophy

WE MAY SAY simply that Jewish philosophy is an attempt to think Judaism through systematically. There was on the whole an important difference between the way the ancient Hebrews thought and the way the ancient Greeks thought. The Greeks tended to classify ideas and examine them in a systematic fashion. The Hebrews seem to have been more interested in the application of ideas to life, in the proper way to live one's life and create a just society.

For instance, there are many passages in the Hebrew Bible dealing with justice. They tell us that God wants man to be fair in his dealings with his neighbors and they also tell us how he should go about doing this: by having just measures, by paying his employees as soon as their wages fall due, by helping those in need, by welcoming the stranger and so forth. But the Hebrews never seem to have discussed, as the Greeks did, such questions as the nature of justice itself.

Most people in the Western world today are the heirs of both the Hebrew and the Greek traditions. We are taught to think systematically from an early age like the Greeks and at the same time the Hebrew Bible has exerted its more direct and concrete influence over us. There is no need for us to try to decide which way is superior, the Hebrew or the Greek, since we now have them both and both can enrich our lives, though without doubt there are areas where the two traditions are in conflict.

For a long period there was little contact between the two ways of thinking. The earliest contact took place during the final centuries before the present era. At that time the Bible was translated into Greek and the Jews of Alexandria in Egypt were Greek speaking (they knew little, if any, Hebrew) and were naturally influenced by Greek ideas. The most important figure of this age was Philo of Alexandria who lived at the very beginning of the present era. Philo was the first to try to harmonize the Hebrew heritage with the Greek. One of the ways he did this was by trying to show that the Bible itself taught many of the ideas familiar to the Greeks and that the Bible, therefore, does not really mean what it often seems to mean. For example, when the Bible tells us that Abraham sent away his wife's handmaiden, Hagar, this is not a very edifying piece of information. Philo consequently understands it to mean that the ideal man, represented by Abraham, has to send away his lust for material possessions or bodily pleasures (represented by Hagar) in order to follow the way of the mind. This was exactly the kind of thing that many of the Greek thinkers had been saying. This method is known as the allegorical method of interpreting Scripture.

Yet until the Middle Ages there was still no real contact between Judaism and Hellenism (as the Greek way is called). Philo was an exception and it is no accident that his name is not mentioned in Jewish literature until as late as the sixteenth century. Jewish thinking as found in the Bible and Talmud went its own way. It developed the Jewish way of life through its great works on Jewish law and through the Midrash it deepened and extended Jewish thought about belief. In the early Middle Ages Arabic translations of the Greek classics found their way into Europe and the Arabic thinkers began to discuss the problems raised for their faith, Islam, by the new Greek learning. The Jews, particularly in lands such as Spain which were under Arabic rule, took to the new ideas and learned much both from the original Greeks and their exponents, the Arabs. Naturally this led them to examine Judaism in the light of Greek and Arabic thought and Jewish philosophy as such was born. Most of the works of the Jewish philosophers at this period were originally written in Arabic, although they were very soon translated into Hebrew.

Since there were very few Hebrew terms for philosophical notions the translators had to invent their terms and this, as well as the difficult and perhaps uncongenial subject matter, has made for neglect, even on the part of learned Jews, of the writings of the medieval Jewish philosophers.

Many works of Jewish philosophy were produced in this period but we need only mention here the more important thinkers whose views are represented in the following pages. The greatest of them all was undoubtedly Moses Maimonides (1135-1204), but he was preceded by Saadiah Gaon (882-942); Bahya ibn Pakuda (eleventh century); and Judah Ha-Levi (eleventh to twelfth century); and followed by Gersonides (1288-1344), Ḥasdai Crescas (1340-1416) and Joseph Albo (c. 1380-c. 1435).

Not all Jews of the Middle Ages thought highly of the new philosophy. Many Jewish teachers felt that the "wisdom of the Greeks" was positively harmful to Jewish faith. What did the Greeks know about God, argued these people. The Greeks did not believe in a revealed Scripture but the Jews did and Jews, by trying to demonstrate all its truth through their own reason, came dangerously close to denying the Torah that God had given. It was sufficient, the opponents of philosophy said, for the good Jew to study his Bible and Talmud and this would equip him to deal with all of life's problems without questioning and probing into matters beyond the scope of the human mind to understand. If, for instance, a Jew believed in God and tried sincerely to do God's will as revealed in the classics of Judaism that was all that God required of him. To go beyond this and try to prove that there is a God (without accepting it on faith and in a spirit of loving trust) could only unsettle his mind and lead him to doubt and eventually to despair.

The followers of philosophy retorted that unless the Jew had trained his mind to think philosophically he would have extremely crude notions on what Judaism was about. He would tend to take literally such Biblical passages which speak of God having a hand, a voice, or an eye and of becoming angry so that he would come to think of God in human terms. Then the Being he worshiped would not be God at all. Then, too, there was the question of authority. The philosophers believed that a man was far more readily prepared to act on the truth if he could see why it was true by working it all out in his own mind. A man was better equipped, they argued, to lead the good life if he knew why it was good rather than accept it blindly by tradition. (The opponents of philosophy retorted that the opposite was true. If the sole support of man's acceptance of the good life was his reasoning powers, these might one day lead him to argue himself out of it all. The real sanction for the good life was unquestioning obedience to the Torah.) One of the followers of philosophy once declared that he was so convinced that this way was right and proper that even if Joshua, the disciple of Moses, came back from heaven to forbid the philosophical way, he would disregard Joshua and continue to study philosophy. After Maimonides' death the Jewish world was split into two camps—the Maimonists, who followed the great sage in embracing philosophy, and the anti-Maimonists who rejected philosophy. After several generations that struggle quieted down, with philosophy becoming a field of interest only for the mature and learned. Other, more pressing problems, harassed the Jewish community. Mysticism, for example, as a more direct approach to the religious life, became popular as a rival to philosophy.

The following selections from the writings of the medieval Jewish philosophers will give you some idea of the kind of topics they discussed and their approach to them. It will be seen that practically all the main problems they considered have to do with the apparent conflict between revelation (as recorded in the Bible) and human reasoning (which had been given its cutting edge by Greek modes of thought). In cases of such conflict it was theoretically possible to reject the Bible in favor of reason, but this solution was almost never adopted by the Jewish thinkers of this period. They, of course, believed that the Bible was revealed by God and could not, therefore, teach anything that was false. There were then two ways open to them when there was a conflict between what reason said in their day and what the Bible taught. They could either re-examine the ideas supposedly based on reason and demonstrate that, in fact, they were mistaken, or re-interpret the Bible so that its teachings did not conflict with reason. Most philosophers used both approaches from time to time though some men seemed to try to justify reason more and others the Bible. Yet in all cases one may say that the underlying belief of these men was that reason and revelation are ultimately harmonious. The Bible and the philosophers are both talking about one truth despite the seeming differences between them. It is the Jewish philosophers' task to draw forth and explain in systematic, intellectual terms, that fundamental unity.

It remains only to be said that the study of philosophy has progressed a good deal since the Middle Ages. Philosophers today would reject some of the arguments advanced by the Greeks, the Arabs and their Jewish followers in this earlier period. For all its distance from us, the attempt the medieval Jewish thinkers made to understand Judaism as a reasonable faith still often speaks to us. It is quite remarkable how, despite the centuries, many of their questions are our questions, many of their problems and arguments are ones we are still working with. Best of all, they give us models of what it is like for men of faith to use the best intellectual tools of their time to explain their Jewish faith and on the basis of their faith not hesitate to challenge modern notions which seem false or injurious.

On doubt and certainty

*Some of the causes by which uncertainty arises
in the minds of men.*

**I want to add to the above my thoughts on the causes of doubt and
denial both of the miracles and of faith in God. It appears to me that
we meet regularly with eight such main causes.**

*Saadiah in his Introduction to his book discusses the whole question
of belief. Toward the end of the Introduction he adds eight main
reasons why men come to deny God. For Saadiah belief in God
is so obvious and true that the fact that there are unbelievers
needs to be explained.*

**The first reason for doubt is that men are naturally reluctant to think
deeply about things. So when they are presented with an idea that
can strengthen their faith in the Torah they run away from it and
are frightened by it. This is why you will find many people saying
that the truth is hard, and some of them saying that the truth is
bitter. Wishing to be free of the whole matter they therefore run
away. Of such persons Scripture says: "Get you far from the Lord!
unto us is this land given for a possession" (Ezekiel 11:15). But these
fools do not see that if they obey their natural inclination to run
away from any effort or labor they will remain hungry and suffer
because of their neglect to sow anything or to build anything.**

The first reason is that men are afraid of the truth because to understand it requires mental effort. Men say, why should I bother my head about such matters? In each of his statements Saadiah skillfully quotes a Scriptural verse from which he tries to show that the Bible anticipated the kind of objection raised. The verse from Ezekiel suggests that some people find it more comfortable and less burdensome to be far from God. After quoting his verse Saadiah in each case points out the flaw in the argument of the unbeliever. Here he says that to run away from the truth because of the effort it involves is to run away from life since nothing worthwhile or creative is possible without effort. Saadiah thus not only thinks about the question of doubt in a systematic way, he also argues against each possible position systematically.

The second reason for doubt is the stupidity which affects many people so that they talk foolishly and tend to think highly of laziness. So whenever a valuable idea is presented to them they satisfy their conscience by declaring there is nothing to it. Regarding such persons Scripture says: "Surely now shall they say: 'We have no king; for we feared not the Lord; and the king, what can he do for us?'" (Hosea 10:3). These people do not consider that by speaking such foolish and arrogant words they perish and die.

The first cause of doubt is hostility to thinking at all about the truth. Here Saadiah says that a second cause is that even when men do think about the truth they often do so in a half-hearted manner and so fail to grasp it. In the verse the king can do much for the people but they dismiss the matter out of hand. Saadiah argues that there is no life worth living unless people are prepared to think things through. Note in each instance Saadiah's method and order: first the reason for doubt, then the Scriptural verse, then the demonstration that the unbeliever's case is unsound.

The third reason for doubt is that man by his nature tends to satisfy his desire for food, drink, sex and possessions so that he busies himself energetically with these without giving any thought to other matters. Regarding such persons Scripture says: "The fool hath said in his heart: 'There is no God'" (Psalms 53:2). Such persons do not consider that if they were to indulge their appetites thoughtlessly

when they are sick, or for that matter even when they are well, they would soon perish.

The third cause of doubt is that men do not want to bother about spiritual matters because they wish to indulge their appetites. The Hebrew word for fool in the verse is naval, and it means just such a person who has no use for spiritual things. Saadiah argues that unless a man learns self control he will do things harmful to himself.

The fourth reason for doubt is that there is too little reflection and too much indifference at the time when a true idea is presented to people or there is insufficient thinking done. People then say to themselves: I have given the matter thought but it means little to me. Regarding such persons Scripture says: "The slothful man shall not hunt his prey" (Proverbs 12:27). The meaning of slothful in this context is one who fails to pursue an idea to its conclusion. Such persons do not see that if they were to behave in this way with regard to things they want they would never attain them.

In the second cause people thought lazily about spiritual matters. Here they think adequately but do not bother to follow the matter to its conclusion.

The fifth reason for doubt is that pride and contempt, once they get hold of man, prevent him from admitting that he is ever ignorant of any wise matter or ever incapable of perceiving any subject. Regarding such persons Scripture says: "The wicked, in the pride of his countenance, saith he will not inquire" (Psalms 10:4). Such persons should appreciate that this kind of attitude will be of no use to one who wishes to fashion a ring or to write even a single letter of a word.

Here a man is so sure that he knows everything that he refuses to acknowledge the truth. He cannot bear to learn anything new because this would be an admission that until then he had been ignorant of it. In the verse quoted, Saadiah stresses the word "inquire." The "wicked" is so proud that he cannot bear to "inquire." T. H. Huxley once described the attitude of the true scientist as a readiness to sit down before the facts like a little child.

*Saadiah points out that unless a man is prepared to learn he
cannot acquire any skills. Craftsmanship and writing are examples
he gives of skills which have to be learned.*

The sixth reason for doubt is that a man hears a word uttered by an unbeliever which touches his heart and wounds it so that his heart remains in its wounded state for the rest of his life. Regarding such persons Scripture says: "The words of a whisperer are as dainty morsels" (Proverbs 18:8). Such persons do not reflect that if they fail to protect themselves against heat and cold these will cause their death.

*Doubt is sometimes caused by some argument of a non-believer
which disturbs faith. But, says Saadiah, one must learn to
protect oneself against such arguments just as one learns to
protect oneself against excess heat and cold.*

The seventh reason for doubt is that a man hears from a believer in God a weak argument in support of his faith. Then he argues, since this is nonsense, all the arguments of believers deserve to be ridiculed. Of such persons Scripture says: "But they laughed them to scorn, and mocked them" (II Chronicles 30:10). Such persons do not consider that the value of choice garments is not affected by the fact that the one who deals in them may not know how to make the most of them when he sells them.

*An obviously weak and ineffectual argument for belief in God is
presented and the person hearing it concludes that every argument
for faith is similarly invalid. But, says Saadiah, the fact that believers
are often unskillful in presenting their valid case is as little reason
for rejecting the case itself as would be a failure to obtain a
bargain in costly garments just because the salesman does not
know how to praise his wares. The Arabic text speaks not of
"costly" garments (as in the Hebrew translation) but of "garments
from Dabik" (a town in Egypt evidently famous for its
valuable cloth). This does not, of course, affect the argument.*

The eighth reason for doubt is when a man hates some believers and this leads him to hate the God in whom they believe. Regarding such persons Scripture says: "My zeal hath undone me, because mine adversaries have forgotten Thy words" (Psalms 119:139). Such foolish persons do not see that a man can do more harm to himself than his enemies can do to him. For a man's enemies have no power to bring upon him eternal pain and sorrow.

Here Saadiah refers to what psychologists today call association. Because a person is hated any opinion he advances is rejected out of hand without any consideration of its truth or falsehood. The verse quoted similarly speaks of a confusion between an opinion and the holder of it. But, says Saadiah, to reject a true opinion merely because it is advanced by an enemy is to do more harm to oneself than anything the enemy can do, particularly when the issue at stake is the knowledge of God upon which man's eternal happiness depends.

It is, however, possible that a man may entertain false beliefs because he noticed in Scripture some verses which seem to be wrong; or because he prayed to God and his prayer was not answered; or he asked something of God and it was not granted to him; or because he observed that God had left unpunished some wicked men; or because he was astonished to witness unbelievers occupying high rank; or because he saw death destroying people indiscriminately; or because his mind was unable to grasp the idea of God's unity or the ideas of the soul and reward and punishment. All these and similar topics I shall mention in due course and in their proper place and I shall explain them to the best of my ability. With God's help I hope that in this way I shall be of benefit to those who are prepared to come along with me.

Saadiah now comes to his aim in writing his book. The causes for unbelief mentioned above are all due to stupidity or folly for which a man can be blamed. But Saadiah now states that, of course, an honest and sincere man may be led into unbelief because belief has not been explained adequately to him and he is honestly puzzled by real difficulties. Such a person can benefit from instruction and Saadiah believes that once he is shown the way of reason such a man will find faith. The rest of his book Saadiah devotes, then, to a reasoned examination of the obstacles to faith. (To put it another way, the eight causes Saadiah has just mentioned are emotional and hence cannot really be argued. But the objections he now states are intellectual and can be argued.)

CHAPTER 12

On creation

How we can prove that the world was created.

Some people say that the universe came into being by chance without having a Creator at the beginning or a Maker who fashioned it. But I am astonished that such an idea should be entertained by any healthy-minded human being.

Bahya has tried to prove in this section of his book that the universe came into being at a given point in time. (This was the philosopher's chief means of proving there was a God.) He now goes on to say that some people argue that even if that is so it does not follow that the universe was created by God. It may just have happened. Bahya replies that such an opinion is absurd. The universe shows evidence of wisdom in its planning and wisdom must come from a mind. This is the Mind of God. This type of argument is known in the history of philosophy as the teleological argument for the existence of God. (Telos is the Greek word for end or purpose. The argument moves from evidence of design or purpose in the universe to the existence of a Designer.) Another name for it is the argument from (or to) design.

Supposing one who puts forward such a view were to hear someone say this: there is a certain waterwheel, which revolves and waters

a portion of a field or a garden. It was set up there without the aid of a skilled craftsman who took the trouble of putting its sections together and arranging each of its parts so that it can fulfill its particular function. Surely one would be greatly surprised at such a suggestion and would treat the person who advanced it as utterly stupid. Without more ado he would prove the statement false and reject it.

Even a simple machine like a waterwheel must be put together so that it can function properly. In the early nineteenth century Paley gave a similar illustration of a watch. Just as it is impossible for the parts of a watch to come together accidentally and function as a watch, so it is impossible for the universe just to have happened. Some later philosophers take issue with this kind of argument on the grounds that you cannot draw conclusions from a tiny part of the universe (a waterwheel or a watch) to the universe as a whole.

Now if such a statement is rejected when made of a small, inferior waterwheel, made by a simple device to water a tiny portion of the earth's surface, how can anyone allow himself to advance it with regard to the great heavenly sphere which revolves around the whole earth and all the creatures upon it? This sphere shows forth wisdom beyond any human comprehension for it is prepared for the benefit of all the earth and all the creatures upon it. How, then, can one suggest that it came into being without a Maker's intention and the thought of an efficient Mind?

The scientific picture of the universe in the Middle Ages when Baḥya wrote his book was of a stationary earth surrounded by spheres. These were thought of as great wheels and the greatest of them all —the great sphere—revolved above and around them with the earth in the center. Another way of describing the spheres was in terms of a gigantic onion with various layers going in different ways. The sun, moon, stars and planets were thought of as fixed in the spheres so that they moved with the spheres. Their astronomy was the science of the movement of these heavenly spheres. Shakespeare in The Merchant of Venice *refers to "the music of the spheres" because it was believed already by the early Greek philosophers that the spheres produced a very subtle melody as they revolved, even though this could not be heard by mortal* ears. Naturally, this picture has now yielded to the much more complex one revealed by modern astronomy. Baḥya clearly adopts the illustration of a revolving waterwheel so as to be able to draw a comparison with the infinitely greater revolutions of the sphere. The Hebrew word for a wheel is galgal and this word is the one used, too, for the great sphere.

It is well known that those things which occur unintentionally do not display the slightest evidence of wisdom or power. You know that if a man suddenly spills ink onto a blank sheet of paper it is impossible for there to appear on that sheet well arranged writing set out in lines which can be read as if they were written with a pen. If a man were to produce a document with the kind of writing only possible when done with a pen and were to claim that the ink spilled over onto the paper so that the writing emerged of its own accord, we would quickly refute him to his face and we would point out that the thing is impossible.

Baḥya now gives a variation of the same argument. Wherever there is evidence of design there is evidence of a designer. Ink spilled accidentally onto a blank sheet of paper does not form itself into meaningful writing; such meaningful writing is conclusive evidence of a writer.

Now if this is impossible even with regard to the forms of letters which, after all, are only significant because of a consensus of opinion, how can we say of something much more refined and whose making is infinitely more profound and far from our understanding that it came into being without a Maker's intention, the wisdom of a Mind, and the power of a Powerful Being?

Baḥya's point about the letters is that the letters of the alphabet are only arbitrary signs, i.e. people agree that A has one sound and meaning, B another and so on and they agree that the letters CAT refer to one thing, the letters DOG to another. Yet if even in the case of letters it is impossible for them just to have happened, how much more so with regard to something so marvelous as the whole universe. This is so particularly because so much wisdom may be directly observed in it, not in the indirect way in which there is wisdom when letters are formed into words and words into sentences.

All that we have said to support the belief in God from an examination of His works is enough for anyone who understands and is sufficient to refute the arguments of the eternalists **who say that matter is eternal.**

This is Baḥya's conclusion to the whole first part of his book (not just to the piece of it quoted here) in which he has refuted the eternalists. Aristotle was the single most influential Greek philosophic thinker of the Middle Ages, particularly in the period after the twelfth century as more of his own writings became available to European thinkers. He was not only important for his ideas and way of thinking, but because he was, so to speak, the father of the science of the Middle Ages. Hence the struggle with Aristotle and the thought which derived from him became critical on many levels to the continuing intellectual respectability of any religion. Baḥya's argument here is typical of the problems involved. He accepts Aristotle's science, that there are heavenly spheres. That, he feels, does not damage or refute his faith. Rather it confirms it. But he rejects Aristotle's idea about the eternity of matter, that it was always there and not created. Apparently he rejected this because it did not seem logical and it would contradict important Jewish teachings. It is not just creation which is at stake, but many other beliefs: the proof that God exists; His control over the universe; His right to command His creatures; the miracles, and other such beliefs.

On suffering in the world

Suffering as part of the order of nature
and why God allows it.

God is the Creator of all living things. He provides them with food and guides them with a wisdom which cannot be fathomed in detail by the human mind but can be grasped in a general sense through observing the workings of nature. This shows that creatures were brought into being intentionally by the will of an All-wise and All-powerful Being.

Judah Ha-Levi's Kuzari *is in the form of a dialogue between the King of the Khazars (a people converted to Judaism) and a Rabbi. The King wishes to know what the teachings of Judaism are before he allows himself and his people to be converted and the Rabbi explains these teachings. In this passage the Rabbi defends God's justice. His argument is that all living creatures are provided with the means to survive and this is evidence of the Creator's wisdom. Ha-Levi says that, of course, we cannot hope to understand God's infinite wisdom in detail but one can witness it at work in a general sense. Centuries later Darwin offered a different explanation of biological development. His theory of evolution saw biological development arising out of survival of the fittest. According to Darwin the giraffe is not endowed with a long neck so that it can reach its food, but giraffes with long necks were able to reach their food and thus survived. Many religious thinkers since Darwin have argued that God's work and wisdom are to be seen in the evolutionary process as a whole.*

These wonders can be seen in the way in which God has endowed all His creatures, great and small, with whatever they need of inward and outward senses, with the spirit of life and with the limbs they require for their survival. He gave to each effective organs suitable to its temperament. For example, He gave power to the hyena and organs with which to maul and tear. He endowed the hare and the stag with a timid nature and gave them the means to escape swiftly. Whoever reflects on each creature's limbs and their use in accordance with its temperament cannot help but see the justice and wisdom with which nature is ordered.

The inward senses are the animal's instincts. The outward senses are, for example, the eagle's capacity to see great distances and the dog's acute sense of hearing and smell.

Suppose someone has a smart idea and points to the injustice involved in the hare becoming the food of the hyena and the fly of the spider. Then man's mind will refute that argument and offer a rebuke saying: How can I possibly attribute injustice to the All-wise Being whose justice is clear to me and who has no need for injustice? If the hyena's capture of the hare and the spider's of the fly were accidental then I would be obliged to support the view that accident rules over everything. But I can see that it is the All-wise who provides the lion with the instruments he needs for the chase, namely, courage and power, teeth and talons. It is the All-wise who provides the spider with its strategy and enables it to weave its web without being instructed how to do this. It is the All-wise who provides the spider with the capacity of weaving its net for the fly and who gives it all the necessary instruments for the purpose. It is the All-wise who provides the fly as food for the spider just as He provides many fish as food for other fish. Can I say of this that it is anything other than incomprehensible wisdom? I must, therefore, acknowledge the justice of the Being of whom it is said: "The Rock whose work is perfect" (Deuteronomy 32:4).

The smart idea is, of course, intended to be ironic. Ha-Levi knows that it is possible to argue that if God is just why does He allow animals to prey on one another. But, he suggests, there is so much of God's wisdom evident in the way in which He provides for His creatures that we are justified in saying that even if we do not understand why God allows animals to prey on one another we can still have faith that somehow this, too, makes sense if only we could understand the mysterious ways in which God works. Ha-Levi is, in fact, saying that we cannot see the answer to the problem of suffering but seeing so much of God's wisdom and goodness we have faith that there is an answer. Man, he says, must not give up in despair and say that everything happens just by chance and that there is no God, for if that were so how do we account for all the evidence we have of God's goodness. We are bothered by the spider catching the fly and are tempted to say that it just happens by accident, but how can such a wonderful thing as a spider's web with all its ingenuity just happen? The sudden change in the passage from hyena to lion is rather puzzling and some texts read "lion" in the whole passage.

Whoever gives thought to this matter will be like Naḥum of Gimzo who used to say about every sorrowful thing that happened to him: "This also is for the best." Such a man will always be happy. He will face suffering with ease and he may even rejoice in suffering if it makes him aware of sins he has committed, like one who pays a debt he owes and is glad that he is rid of it. He will rejoice in the reward and recompense stored up for him and also in the opportunity he has of teaching people to be patient and to acknowledge God's righteousness. He will rejoice, too, in the good name and reputation he acquires.

Naḥum of Gimzo lived in Palestine at the beginning of the second century and was the teacher of the famous Rabbi Akiva. There is a Rabbinic pun on the name Gimzo, the name of a town, so that it is read as gam zo, "this, also." According to tradition Naḥum always used to say when he met with suffering: "This also is for the best," i.e. God knows what He is doing and even the evil in life has some good purpose although we cannot always see what this is. Ha-Levi here suggests four possible virtues to suffering: 1) Suffering is the atonement for our sins; 2) It helps us attain life after death; 3) It makes us an example to others; 4) It gives us a good name

*in society. Not everyone will agree with Ha-Levi that it is right for
the pious sufferer to rejoice "in the good name and reputation he
acquires." While this passage is entirely passive in the face of
whatever happens, perhaps one should balance it with the activism
which is implicit in doing the Commandments. That is not mentioned
here but is the context in which this passage must be seen.*

**This is how he will behave in relation to his own personal troubles
and he will behave in this way, too, in relation to the troubles of
the community. When the thought of Israel's exile and its dispersion
and all its loss and poverty confuses his mind he will, at first, find
comfort in acknowledging God's justice, as we have said. He will
then reflect on the means this offers for payment of sin and on the
reward stored up in the World to Come and on the attachment to
the divine idea in this world.**

*Ha-Levi says that this method of coping with life's troubles can apply
also to general suffering, that of the Jewish people, for example. In
Ha-Levi's day the majority of Jews had a very hard time of it.
Ha-Levi's view is that Israel's sufferings are an atonement for their
sins and they will go to heaven when they die. And even in this
world, for all their sufferings, they have the tremendous privilege
of knowing God—the "divine idea."*

**If the perverse thought causes him to give up hope of all this ever
happening (as it is said: "Can these bones live?" [Ezekiel 37:3] since
we have been cut off from being a nation and our past is forgotten,
as it is said: "Our bones are dried up, and our hope is lost; we are
clean cut off" [Ezekiel 37:11]) he should reflect on the Exodus from
Egypt and on all the events mentioned in the hymn: "For how many
favors do we owe gratitude to God." It will not then seem hard to
believe it possible for us to recover our greatness even after only
one of us has been left alive. As it is said: "Fear not, thou worm
Jacob" (Isaiah 41:14). For what is left of a man once he has become
a worm in his grave?**

*Already in the days of Ezekiel there were Jews who thought that
there was no hope for their people. The prophet, in his famous
vision of the dry bones which lived again, gives the lie to this
pessimism. The hymn Ha-Levi refers to is the Passover hymn Dayenu,*

*still recited at the Seder, in which God is praised for His many
kindnesses to Israel and these are listed. Ha-Levi offers an ingenious
and novel interpretation of the verse about the worm. He takes it
to mean that just as a man can be brought back from the dead by
God's miraculous power even if nothing but a single worm is left of
what was once his body so, too, can "Jacob" (the people of Israel)
be restored even if only one Jew had been left. There is probably
a reference, too, to the theme of the "dry bones."*

CHAPTER 14

The world to come

A description of life in the world to come.

The good that is stored up for the righteous is the life of the World to Come. This is life without death and good without evil. Scripture says of it: "That it may be well with thee, and that thou mayest prolong thy days" (Deuteronomy 22:7). Tradition interprets this to mean: "That it may be well with thee," in the world in which there is only good; "and that thou mayest prolong thy days," in the world which is without end, namely, the World to Come. The reward of the righteous is that they attain to this delight and live with this goodness. The retribution of the wicked is that they do not merit this kind of life but are cut off from it and die. Whoever does not merit this kind of life is dead in that he does not live forever but is cut off in his wickedness to perish like the beasts. This is the meaning of the Biblical term "to be cut off."

This selection is taken from Maimonides' famous code of laws. He could not strictly separate law from ideas. So too his great philosophic work concludes with an extensive section on ethics. Thus the two streams merge with one another. Maimonides, as a philosopher, could not accept literally all the descriptions of heaven and hell in earlier Jewish literature because for him only the spirit of man lives on after death and all the descriptions must consequently be understood in a spiritual sense. He appears also to have been bothered by the many crude descriptions of hell as a place of torment. Hence he advances the novel view that hell is not a place of punishment at all but that the soul of the wicked is simply annihilated at death so that it does not enjoy the bliss of heaven (the World to Come). Maimonides states that the Biblical references to the soul being "cut off" (karet in Hebrew) refer to this.

There are neither bodies nor bodily forms in the World to Come but only the disembodied souls of the righteous who have become like the ministering angels. Since there are no bodies there is no eating or drinking there nor is there anything which the human body needs in this world. Nor does there occur there any of the events which occur to the human body in this world such as sitting, standing, sleep, death, distress, laughter and so forth. The ancient sages say: "In the World to Come there is no eating or drinking or procreation but the righteous sit with their crowns on their heads and bask in the radiance of the Divine Presence." Now when they say "the righteous sit" they mean this in a figurative sense, namely, the righteous exist there without effort or toil. So, too, when they speak of "their crowns on their heads" they refer to the knowledge the righteous acquired by virtue of which they attained to the life of the World to Come. This is with them there and this is their "crown," just as it says: "Even the crown wherewith his mother hath crowned him" (Song of Songs 3:11). Behold Scripture says: "And everlasting joy shall be upon their heads" (Isaiah 51:11). Now joy is not a physical thing that it can rest bodily on a person's head. In the same way the reference of the sages to a "crown" is to knowledge. What is meant by "and bask in the radiance of the Divine Presence"? This means that the righteous know and comprehend the truth regarding the Holy One, blessed be He, in a way they could not know while still in the dark and lowly body.

The "ancient sages" are the scholars, mentioned in the Babylonian Talmud, in the third century. Actually the saying Maimonides quotes is attributed in the Talmud to only one scholar, Rav. Maimonides faces here the difficulty that if there are no bodily events in heaven what can the reference to "sitting" mean and how can there be "crowns" there or, for that matter, "heads"? He replies that these, too, have to be understood metaphorically. The good man, by his noble living and high thinking in this life, has acquired some faint knowledge of God and this is the "crown" referred to while "sitting" means absence of effort. Maimonides then quotes the two Scriptural verses in which similar metaphorical expressions are used. Maimonides believed with the Greeks that the light of the soul is to a large extent darkened by the body. It cannot shine in its full splendor while in the body.

Wherever there is a reference to the "soul" in this context it is not to the psyche which needs the body for its existence but to the form of the soul. This is the knowledge of the Creator which the soul acquired according to its capacity and its comprehension of abstract matters and so forth. This is the form whose nature we have described in the fourth chapter of the Laws of the Principles of the Torah. **It is to this that the term "soul" is applied in this context. This kind of life—since there is no death in it, for death is a bodily event and there are no bodies there—is called "the bundle of life," as it is said: "The soul of my lord shall be bound in the bundle of life" (I Samuel 25:29). This is the reward than which there is none higher and the good than which there is none greater and it is for this that all the prophets longed.**

Maimonides refers here (and in the earlier chapter of his work to which he here refers) to an idea, going back to Plato. The ordinary life force of man, that which enables him to exist, think and feel is not the true "soul" of man. The real "soul" is what Maimonides calls the "form" of the soul. This is a power, independent of the body, to know God and abstract metaphysical truths. Maimonides believed that this "form" is strengthened by living the good life and engaging in profound thought and it is this which is immortal and does not die when the body dies. Some Jewish philosophers disagreed with Maimonides on this point because they felt that it was attributing too much to man's intellect. A good man, they argued, who never had the intellectual capacity for thinking profound thoughts, is as much entitled to go to heaven as his more gifted neighbor. Or, as Professor Leon Roth put it, one does not have to take a philosophy degree in goodness before one can go to heaven.

This reward is called metaphorically by many names: "The mountain of the Lord and His holy place" (Psalms 24:3); "The way of holiness" (Isaiah 35:8); "The courts of the Lord" (Psalms 92:14); "The graciousness of the Lord" (Psalms 27:4); and "The tabernacle of the Lord" (Psalms 15:1). The sages, speaking metaphorically, call this goodness prepared for the righteous a feast. And generally they call it the World to Come.

Maimonides now draws on a number of Scriptural verses which, he claims, refer in metaphorical language to the World to Come. The Rabbis say that in the World to Come God will prepare a great feast for the righteous. Since Maimonides has been at pains to stress that there is no food or drink in heaven he is bound to take this saying, too, metaphorically. There will be a feast of knowledge. Abraham ibn David, Maimonides' famous critic (whose criticisms are generally printed in the texts of Maimonides' work) objects that the Rabbis go on to say that at the end of the feast a cup of wine will be given to King David who will recite Grace after Meals and this seems to suggest that the feast is to be understood literally. No doubt Maimonides would have explained this, too, in a spiritual sense. This passage is typical of much of Maimonides' philosophy. He regularly seeks to explain the meaning of many Biblical terms which appear to be intellectually unacceptable. He does this by showing what he believes the terms really mean.

The retribution than which there is no worse is for the soul to be cut off so that it does not merit this life of the World to Come. As it is said: "That soul shall be utterly cut off, his iniquity shall be upon him" (Numbers 15:31). This destruction is referred to metaphorically by the prophets when they speak of "the nethermost pit" (Psalms 55:24); "destruction" (Psalms 88:12); "a hearth" (Isaiah 30:33); "The horseleech" (Proverbs 30:15) and they call it by every name signifying waste and destruction since it is the destruction out of which there is no reconstruction and the loss which can never be restored.

Maimonides was also criticized for the attempt to deny that there is a hell in which the wicked are tormented but he appears to reject the doctrine, interpreting the Scriptural verses which were said to refer to it as referring to the soul being "cut off" but not suffering eternal torture. Again note the numerous terms "explained."

You may despise this kind of goodness, imagining that the only worthwhile reward for keeping the Commandments and for a man being perfect in the ways of truth is for him to eat and drink well and have beautiful women and wear garments of fine linen and embroidery and live in marble palaces and have vessels of silver and gold and so forth as hold the stupid and perverted Arabs who are immersed in lewdness. But the sages and the intellectuals know that these things are vain and nonsensical and have no value and are only great goods for us in this world where we have bodies and bodily form. All these things have to do with the needs of the body. The soul only longs for them because the body requires them if it is to remain healthy and fulfill its function. But all these things cease when there is no longer a body in existence. There is no way at all for us in this world to know or comprehend the great goodness which the soul experiences in the World to Come, for in this world we know only of material pleasures and it is these we desire. That good is exceedingly great and can only be compared to the good of this world by analogy, but in reality there can be no way of comparing the good of the soul in the World to Come with the physical goods of food and drink in this world. That good is great beyond all our understanding and incomparable beyond all our imagination. Therefore David said: "Oh how great is Thy goodness, which Thou hast laid up for them that fear Thee" (Psalms 31:20).

Maimonides now faces the objection that if heaven is to be understood only in a spiritual sense the reward is too abstract for it to have any appeal. Maimonides does not deny that for us in this life only material pleasures have a strong appeal but, he argues, this is because we have bodies. But in the spiritual life of the World to Come we shall have only souls and these have their own purely spiritual delights. We are, in fact, incapable of appreciating a pure spiritual delight, so words speaking of material pleasures have to be used even when describing spiritual bliss. But, says Maimonides, we must never mistake the metaphor for the reality. In another of his works Maimonides says that for people on earth to understand pure spiritual bliss is as futile as the attempt of a man born blind to understand the nature of color. The reference to the Arabs is to certain Islamic believers who held that in heaven there will be material pleasures. Maimonides ridicules this notion.

How David longed for the life of the World to Come and how he desired it! As it is said: "If I had not believed to look upon the goodness of the Lord in the land of the living!" (Psalms 27:13). The ancient sages have already told us that man is incapable of really comprehending the good of the World to Come and that only the Holy One, blessed be He, Himself knows its greatness, beauty and nature and that all the good things the prophets predicted for Israel refer only to the material pleasures which will be theirs in the days of the Messiah when Israel will again have dominion. But there is nothing to which the life of the World to Come can be compared and it is beyond the human imagination. The prophets did not try to imagine it lest their imagination make it less than it really is. The sages say: All the prophets only prophesied for the days of the Messiah but as for the World to Come: "Eye hath not seen it save Thou O God" (Isaiah 64:3).

Maimonides is aware that the prophets speak of happiness in the future in physical terms and it is difficult to go so far as to explain these metaphorically. His reply is based on a saying in the Talmud that all these things refer only to the Messianic age, which is on earth, but in the World to Come there is only spiritual bliss. The Rabbis often speak of the World to Come. According to the majority of commentators the reference is to the "resurrection of the dead" i.e. at some time in the future all the dead will arise from their graves to live again on this earth. But Maimonides considered such a concept too materialistic (though in a letter on the subject he wrote toward the end of his life he said that he did not deny that the dead would live again for a time on earth but it would not be forever). He prefers to understand the Rabbinic references to the World to Come as a spiritual state which the soul enjoys after the death of the body. He also deals with the question often raised in the Middle Ages as to why there are no references to heaven in the prophetic books. His reply is the ingenious one that even the prophet has never been there and if he were to refer to heaven he would be obliged to rely on his imagination and this he does not wish to do because all human imagination must fall far short of the reality.

When the sages call it the World to Come this does not mean that it is not now in existence so that when this world is destroyed that

World will come into being. This is not so. But it is in existence all the time, as it is said: "Which Thou hast laid up for them that fear Thee" (Psalms 31:20). They only called it the World to Come because that type of life only comes to man after he first experiences the life of this world in which we exist with a body as well as a soul.

Maimonides concludes that this spiritual state called the World to Come is already here, as it were. It is laid up for those who fear God. But since man cannot experience it while he has a body it is spoken of as something yet to come.

On praising God

The limits of what we may meaningfully say about God.

Even that which lies in our power to know about God, we can know only by means of negation. Everyone agrees to that. But through negation we can never know anything about the true nature of that from which the negation is made. So all thinkers, past and present, agree that the human mind cannot comprehend God. Only God can know Himself. The only form of comprehension of God we can have is to realize how futile it is to try to comprehend Him.

Maimonides holds what is known in the history of religious philosophy as the doctrine of negative attributes. An attribute is something we say of God e.g. that He is good or wise. Maimonides holds that the true nature of God is so far beyond the grasp of the human mind that it is derogatory to God to use human terms when speaking about Him. We must not, therefore, say that God is good if we mean by this that we are saying something positive about His nature (positive attributes). Why, then, do we say that God is good? For Maimonides this can only mean that we negate from Him the opposite of good. When we say that God is good we mean that although His true nature cannot be known, we do know that He is not the opposite of good. So with all the attributes. They tell us what God is not. That is the way of "negation." It follows therefore that all we can know about God is that we cannot know what He is, that is, what His true nature is, for that is known

only to Him. We can know what He is not and that never makes
God less than He is and yet is very helpful to man to know.
In the history of religious thought this doctrine is also called
the via negativa, "the way of negation."

**All philosophers say: "He has overcome us with His pleasantness
but is hidden from us by the power of His appearance, just as the
sun remains hidden to eyes too weak to gaze at it." They have written a good deal on this subject but there is no point in repeating
here all that they have said.**

The sun, by its very power and splendor, prevents us from gazing
at it and hence we cannot really know it. So it is with God,
say the philosophers.

**The most extreme thing that can be said in this matter is found in
the book of Psalms (65:2): "Silence is praise to Thee." This means:
With regard to Thee it is praise if one remains silent. This is a very
powerful statement of the theme. For anything positive we say with
the intention of praising and magnifying God contains something
applicable to Him but also something derogatory to Him. It is therefore better to remain silent and content oneself with contemplation
in the mind. As the perfect teachers say: "Commune with your own
heart upon your bed, and be still" (Psalms 4:5).**

Whenever something is said of God, such as that He is good or wise,
there is some truth in the saying (He is not the opposite) but also
much untruth (since these terms are human and cannot really
be applied to God). The best thing would be, therefore, to think
about God but not to say anything positive about Him.

**You know the famous saying of the Rabbis (if only all sayings would
be of such value) which I shall here quote in the form they expressed
it. I am aware that everyone knows it but I want to call your attention to its meaning.**

The saying Maimonides quotes is found in the Babylonian Talmud,
tractate Berakhot 33b. Maimonides' purpose in quoting it at length
is in order to discuss the obvious question: If silence is to be
preferred why do we, in fact, praise God in our prayers?

A certain person, leading the services in the presence of Rabbi Hanina, said: "God, the great, the valiant and the tremendous, the powerful, the strong and the mighty." Rabbi Hanina chided him: "Have you now exhausted all the praises of your Master? We would not even be allowed to say 'The great, the valiant and the tremendous' if Moses had not recorded these in the Torah and if the Men of the Great Synagogue had not ordained their use in prayer, and yet you dare to say all this! A parable can be given. A king of flesh and blood possessed millions of gold coins but was praised for possessing millions of silver coins. Was not this an attempt to disgrace him?" This is the saying of the saint.

The first thing we notice is how Rabbi Hanina silenced the reader and rejected the increase of positive attributes. Consider how he showed that if we were left to ourselves we would never dare to utter any of the attributes and we would not have spoken anything of them.

In Talmudic times a reader of the prayers in public would often compose his own prayers in addition to the standard ones. The three attributes of God which we are enjoined to use in prayer were uttered by Moses (Deuteronomy 10:7). The Men of the Great Synagogue were the teachers after the Return from the Babylonian exile who were said to have flourished in the fifth century B.C.E. According to the tradition, they were the authors of the Eighteen Benediction prayers (still said today) at the beginning of which these attributes are mentioned: Ha-El ha-Gadol, ha-Gibbor v'ha-Nora.

However, something must be said if human beings are to have some faint picture. As the Rabbis say: "The Torah speaks in the language of men." So the tradition depicts the Creator in terms of human perfection. Yet it should be our aim to limit our use of such utterances, using attributes of God only when we read them in the Torah. When the Men of the Great Synagogue, who were prophets, came along, they ordained that the three attributes might be mentioned in prayer. It should be our aim to limit our words only to these when we pray.

Maimonides says that Moses had to say something because human beings have a psychological need to give expression in speech to their worship of God in order to have "some faint picture" (i.e. not the real truth) of the God they worship. "The Torah speaks in the language of men" is a Rabbinic saying. Maimonides uses it to explain that since we cannot use divine language of God we have to use human language. But we must always remember that this is really inapplicable to God. The idea here is that a prophet like Moses can tell us what human language to use and only a prophet can do this. But according to the tradition there were prophets among the Men of the Great Synagogue (e.g. Haggai, Zechariah and Malachi) and they tell us that this language can also be used in our prayers. It follows that no other attribute may be used, hence the Rabbi's rebuke of the reader.

The main point of the passage is to tell us that two conditions have to be satisfied before we can use attributes in our prayers. The first is that they must be found in the Torah. The second is that the prophets must have ordained their use in prayer. Were it not for the first condition we would not be allowed to use them at all and were it not for the second condition we would not be allowed to remove them from their context to use them in our prayers. "Yet, you dare to say all this!"

From this you can see that it is not right for us to use in our prayers all the attributes of God found in the books of the prophets. For Rabbi Ḥanina did not simply say that if Moses had not used them we could not have used them but he went on to imply that we can use them only because the Men of the Great Synagogue so ordained.

Here Maimonides states that it is not only wrong to use our own attributes (as the reader did) but also to use those found in the prophetic books. Although the prophets used them it is necessary before we can use them to have the sanction of the Men of the Great Synagogue. Otherwise why did Rabbi Ḥanina have to bring in the Men of the Great Synagogue at all? It would have been enough that a prophet (Moses) had used them.

We must not follow those really stupid people who are fond of increasing God's attributes in prayer, composing hymns and poems by which, according to their way of thinking, they can draw near to

God. They go so far as to describe God in terms which would be an offense even if used of human beings. For they have no understanding of these great and important topics, so remote from the popular mind. Treating God as a means of exercising their poetic skill, they use attributes and speak of Him in any way they see fit and keep piling on praises thinking this will have an effect on Him.

Because of his strict views here Maimonides (like some other Jewish thinkers of his age) had a poor opinion of the hymn makers (the writers of piyyutim) who tended to use human language unrestrainedly in speaking of God.

How much more so if they discover something of the kind in the words of the prophets. Failing to see that such passages have to be explained, they take them literally and then allow themselves to derive other expressions from those used by the prophets, permitting their exercise to branch off into different ways and constructions.

Expressions found in the prophetic books are not to be taken literally as the poets do when they "lift" these expressions and use them in their compositions. Worse, they use them as a basis for creating new descriptions of their own.

This kind of license is particularly to be observed among the poets and composers of hymns and among those who imagine that they are poets. Some of the results are real heresy and others are so stupid and unimaginative that they make a person laugh when first he hears them and later weep that such things should be said of God.

If it were not that I pity these men I would tell you something about their compositions so that you would appreciate their faults. But the faults are really obvious to anyone who gives thought to the matter.

Say to yourself, if slander is a great offense how much more is a loose tongue applied to God by attributing to Him things far below Him. I do not suggest that there is conscious rebellion against God in this matter but unintentional blasphemy is certainly present both on the part of the public which hears them and the fools who compose them.

However, anyone aware of the fault of such sayings who continues to use them is, to my way of thinking, one of those of whom it was said: "And the children of Israel used words that were not right against the Lord their God" (II Kings 17:9) and "utter error against the Lord" (Isaiah 32:6).

If you are one of those who respect God's glory you must never listen to such things, still less utter them, and still less compose them. You know only too well how great an offense it is to utter arrogant things when speaking to God.

Never in any circumstances should you allow yourself to use positive attributes of God in order to magnify Him in your mind. Never go beyond that which the Men of the Great Synagogue ordained for use in prayer and blessing. This is enough for your needs and more than enough, as Rabbi Ḥanina has said.

Everything else which you find in the prophetic books, read when you come across it but look upon it, as we have earlier explained, either as a description of God's deeds or to teach that the opposite must be negated of God. This, too, is not for publication to the masses. This type of contemplation is only for the few for whom God's greatness does not consist in saying of Him improper things but in understanding about Him proper things.

Maimonides adds here something he has explained elsewhere in his book. The prophets do use positive attributes at times but these are either intended in a negative sense or else they do not refer to God at all but to His deeds. On this latter view when we say that God is compassionate we mean that He performs compassionate acts. This still says nothing about His nature which is beyond our comprehension. We can, however, speak positively about God as long as we are willing to talk only about what He does, not about what He is. All this is, however, too hard for ordinary people to comprehend.

We complete our observations on the wise words of Rabbi Ḥanina. He does not give the parable of the king who had *millions* of gold coins but who was praised for having *hundreds* of gold coins. For this would suggest that God's perfections, though far greater than those actually attributed to Him, are yet of the same kind. This is not so, as we have earlier proved.

The wisdom of the parable consists in the statement that the king had millions of *gold* coins and was praised for having millions of *silver* coins. This is to teach us that those things which for us are perfections cannot be attributed to God at all and that for Him they are imperfections, as he goes on to say: "Was this not an attempt to disgrace him?"

It is not that God is different from us in degrees of perfection but that all human perfection is different in kind from divine perfection. As far as His nature is concerned, God is different from us not merely in a quantitative way but in a qualitative one.

So I have now explained to you that whatever perfections you find in attributes used of humans are imperfections if applied to God in that same sense. Solomon has given us enough right teaching on the subject when he said: "For God is in heaven, and thou upon earth; therefore let thy words be few" (Ecclesiastes 5:1).

The book of Ecclesiastes was attributed to King Solomon. Notice how skillfully Maimonides uses the verse to suggest that since there is such a great divide between "heaven" and "earth" one's words should be few when speaking of heavenly matters.

CHAPTER 16

MAIMONIDES: YAD HA-ḤAZAKAH, "THE STRONG HAND," TESHUVAH, V

Is man free? PART I

God's will that man should have free will.

Man can please himself. If he wishes to turn to the good way and be righteous he can do so and if he wishes to turn to the evil way and be wicked he can do so. This is the meaning of the verse: "Behold man is unique in that good and evil depend on him alone" (Genesis 3:22). This means that the human species is unique. No other species in the world has the property man has. Of his own accord and knowledge and thinking he knows good and evil. He can do whatever he wishes and no one can prevent him from doing either good or evil. Since this is so: "lest he put forth his hand" (Genesis 3:22).

Maimonides quotes the verse in Genesis but gives it a very different meaning from the usual one. The Hebrew words k'aḥad mimmennu (English translation: "as one of us") he translates as "unique" (k'aḥad) in that it is from him (mimmennu) to know good and evil. He connects this with the first words of the next phrase "V'ata pen yishlaḥ yado"—"and now lest he put forth his hand." Thus Maimonides connects the ability to know with the power to control one's actions. Adam acquired the sort of knowledge which enabled him to be the determiner of his behavior.

Do not permit yourself to argue, as do the foolish nations of the world and the majority of unsophisticated Jews, that God decrees

at the beginning of man's creation whether he will be righteous or wicked. This is not so. Every man can be as righteous as Moses or as wicked as Jeroboam, foolish or kind or cruel or niggardly or generous or have any other such traits of character without any one compelling him or decreeing so or propelling him to either one of the two ways open to him. He himself, of his own accord, can turn in the direction he pleases. This is why Jeremiah says: "Out of the mouth of the Most High proceedeth not evil and good" (Lamentations 3:38). This means that God does not ordain that a man be good or evil. Since this is so a sinner has only himself to blame. Consequently it is right for him to weep and mourn over his sins and for harming his own self. Therefore it is written in the next verse: "Wherefore doth a living man complain, a strong man because of his sins" (Lamentations 3:39). Jeremiah goes on to say, since we can please ourselves and since all the evil we do is of our own accord it is right that we repent and leave aside our wickedness for the power to do so is now in our own hands. Hence it is written in the next verse: "Let us search and try our ways, and return to the Lord" (Lamentations 3:40).

The "foolish nations" probably means the Muslims whose philosophy was fatalistic i.e. that whatever happens is fated by God and it cannot be otherwise. The "unsophisticated Jews" followed this belief. To this day many Jews speak of things being fated but Maimonides would disapprove. Jeroboam in the Jewish tradition is an example of great wickedness (see I Kings 11:26-13:34) because he not only sinned himself but caused others to sin. The verse Maimonides quotes from the book of Lamentations was attributed to the prophet Jeremiah.

This is a great principle and a pillar upon which rest the Torah and the Commandments. As it is said: "See, I have set before thee this day life" (Deuteronomy 30:15). And it is written: "Behold, I set before you this day" (Deuteronomy 11:26), namely, the power lies in your own hands. Whatever a man wishes to do of the things men do, whether good or evil, he can do. It is on the basis of this idea that Scripture says: "Oh that they had such a heart" (Deuteronomy 5:26), that is to say, God does not force human beings to do good or evil nor does He decree this for them but it is all left to them.

The verse: "Oh that they had such a heart" suggests that God yearns, as it were, for people to be good but does not force them to be good. It all depends on the people themselves.

If it were true, as the stupid believers in astrology have invented, that God determines whether a man will be good or evil, or if it were true that there is something which forces a man from birth in the direction of a certain way or philosophy or to have certain traits of character or to perform certain deeds, how can God command us through His prophets: Do this and do not do that, mend your ways and do not persist in your wickedness. It would have already been determined what he is to do from the moment of birth or he would be forced from birth to follow a way from which he could not escape. What would be the point of the whole Torah if this were true and by what justice would the sinner be punished and the righteous rewarded? Shall the Judge of all the earth not deal justly?

Do not be astonished so that you argue: How is it possible that man be free to do whatever he wills and for his deeds to be in his own hands? Can man do anything at all without God's permission and will? But surely it is written: "Whatsover the Lord pleased, that hath He done, in heaven and in earth" (Psalms 135:6). You must know that God does whatever He wills even though our deeds are in our own hands. How can this be? God willed fire and water to go upward, water and earth to go downward, the spheres to move in a circle and other creatures of the world to follow the pattern He has set for them. So, too, He willed for man to have free will and for his deeds to be in his own hands without him being forced or driven. He himself, by means of the intelligence God has given him, can do all he wishes to do. This is why man is judged according to his deeds. If he does good then good is done to him and if evil then evil is done to him. This is what the prophet means when he says: "This hath been of your doing" (Malachi 1:9) and "According as they have chosen their own ways" (Isaiah 66:3). It is in this connection that Solomon says: "Rejoice, O young man, in thy youth . . . But know thou, that for all these things God will bring thee into judgment" (Ecclesiastes 11:9). This means: Know that you have the power to do as you please and you must therefore give account to God in the future for whatever you do.

Maimonides was one of the very few Jewish thinkers in the Middle Ages who rejected a belief in astrology. The astrologers claimed that the way the stars appeared in the heavens at the time of man's birth determines his character. Astrology claimed the status of a science in that period and it had the support of most of the intelligent men of the era. Maimonides, with great courage, rejects astrology as sheer superstition and argues here that if this is true how can the prophets urge men to be good if it all depends on the stars. Shakespeare (Julius Caesar I, 11, 134) similarly says:

"The fault, dear Brutus, is not in our stars,
But in ourselves, that we are underlings."

To the question, how can anything be done without God's will? Maimonides replies that it is precisely God's will that man should have free will. The book of Ecclesiastes is traditionally attributed to King Solomon.

You might ask the following question. God knows everything. Therefore before a man is born does God know or not know whether he is to be good or bad? And if God does know that he is to be good it is then impossible for him to be anything but good! If you argue that although God does know that he will be good it is still possible for him to be bad, then God does not really know. You must appreciate that the answer to this question is longer than the earth and wider than the sea and that many great mountains of faith depend upon it. It is vital for you to understand what I am about to say. We have already explained, in the second chapter of the Laws of the Foundations of the Torah, that God does not know with a knowledge that is separate from Himself like human beings. For humans self and knowledge are two separate things. But in God, may He be exalted, name and knowledge are one. It is not given to humans to understand this matter fully. Just as no human being is able to discover the true nature of the Creator, as it is said: "Man shall not see Me and live" (Exodus 33:20), so too no human being can comprehend and discover the Mind of the Creator. The prophet refers to this when he says: "For My thoughts are not your thoughts, neither are your ways My ways" (Isaiah 55:8). Since this is so we cannot understand how God can know all creatures and every deed.

But we can know without doubt that man's deeds are in his own hands and God does not drive him to do them or decree that he should do them. It is not only because of our tradition that we know this to be so but by means of clear scientific proof. Because this is so, prophecy states that man is judged by his deeds and according to his deeds, whether good or bad. This is a principle upon which depends all the words of prophecy.

Maimonides here states the most acute philosophical problem of the Middle Ages and, for that matter, one unresolved to this day. Judaism has traditionally taught that God knows everything before it happens and that there can be no limit to His knowledge. (In philosophical language this is expressed by saying that God is omniscient). Now this must mean that God knows what a man will do before the man is born and if this is so how can the man help doing that which God knows he will do? It will not do to say that God knows that he may do this or that, for this would not be knowledge. Maimonides does not give a complete answer. Indeed his solution is that this very difficult matter cannot possibly be understood by the human mind. What Maimonides tries to do is to show why this must be so. When a human being knows something he and the thing he knows are separate. For instance, if I know that two and two make four, it is my I which knows this and the thing known is not me. In learning it I make it part of me. But this cannot be said of God, for nothing can be added to God, even by His knowing something else. We are obliged to say (and Maimonides has discussed this, as he says, elsewhere) that in God knowledge and self are one. From this it follows that to know what is meant by God's knowledge is to know God's true nature and this is impossible for man. Consequently, while it is true that if a human being knows what another human being will do, logically we may say that the second person has no choice but to do it. Maimonides says this is not true of God's knowledge, which is too wonderful to be defined or understood. Simply put: God's mind is not only greater but grander than man's. But that rests everything on faith. Some thinkers have tried to deal with the problem by arguing that God knows past, present and future at once. All God's knowledge is present and thus does not include foreknowledge but does include freedom. It may be that Maimonides is thinking of a similar solution. Abraham ibn David, Maimonides' critic, remarks that Maimonides should not have raised the question if he knew that he had no answer because the question might unsettle people and lead them to have religious doubts. Maimonides finally states that we know that man is free not only because of our religious tradition (i.e. we do not have to accept it purely as a matter of faith) but it can be proved scientifically, that is to say by an appeal to human reason. What is proved is that man has free will, not that free will is compatible with divine omniscience.

Is man free? PART II

The possibilities of freedom open to man.

By means of rational thought we have reached the opinion that God knows in advance only the possibilities open to a man in his freedom, not the particular decisions he will make. Now it is right for us to explain that this is also the view of our Torah. It is clearly the cornerstone of the Torah or the axis upon which it pivots that there are *possible* things. This is why the Torah commands us to do certain things and to refrain from doing other things.

Gersonides disagrees with Maimonides' view mentioned earlier. Gersonides argues that if man is truly free to do certain things it is impossible that God should know them beforehand. He therefore advances the startling view that while God knows the whole order of a man's life (i.e. God knows the different possibilities open to man) He does not know how men will, in fact, choose in particular circumstances since man has the power to choose between the possibilities open to him. Gersonides believes that not only is his view the only rational one, but that it accords with the words of the Scripture. He begins here by saying that the Torah clearly recognizes the existence of possibilities i.e. that God knows some things not as certainties but as possibilities. When the Torah orders man to be just, for instance, this can only mean that the possibility is open to man to be unjust, otherwise what is the point of the command? Because of his radical views, such as this one, many Rabbis urged their pupils to refrain from reading Gersonides' works. Nonetheless

*he was acknowledged as a great, if daring, Jewish thinker. This
is a good example of the kind of freedom Judaism permitted
in the realm of ideas and thought.*

It is a cornerstone of the words of the prophets, on whom be peace,
that God informs the prophets of these *possible* things before they
happen, as they say: "For the Lord God will do nothing, but He
revealeth His counsel unto His servants the prophets" (Amos 3:7).
The prophets also teach that even when they foretell evil it is not
determined that the evil they foretell will actually happen, as they
say: "For the Lord is gracious and repenteth Him of the evil" (Joel
2:13).

*Gersonides argues that there appears to be a contradiction in the
words of the prophets. Sometimes they say that this or that will
happen and yet say that it is possible for it not to happen.*

Now it is impossible to reconcile these two points of view (that on
the one hand the prophets say in the name of God that things will
happen and yet on the other hand they teach that they may not
happen) unless it is postulated that these *possibilities* are ordered
from one point of view (and from this point of view it can be said
that God knows them) and not ordered from another point of view
(and from this point of view they are only *possibilities* even to God)
and that God knows all this. Since they are ordered by Him, God
knows them as *possibilities*. It follows that the view of our Torah
with regard to God's foreknowledge is the same as that at which we
arrive by the exercise of our rational thought.

*The point Gersonides makes here is that when the prophets declare
that a thing will happen they do not mean that it is already fixed
and certain. If this were so how could they go on to say that it
may not happen? Gersonides' solution is that the original declaration
is that things have been so ordered by God; that this event is a
possibility for this particular man (and this they declare with
certainty), but he still has the power to choose and in this sense it
is uncertain because the actual outcome is uncertain.*

A further proof that, according to our Torah, God knows these
matters in a general, not a particular, sense is the verse: "He that

fashioneth the hearts of them all together, that giveth heed to all their works" (Psalms 33:15). This means that God has fashioned the hearts and thoughts of men *together* by arranging the order produced by the heavenly bodies by means of which the lives of men are ordered in a general sense. It is in this sense that He "giveth heed to all their works," namely, in the sense of *together,* not that His knowledge embraces every particular. So it is clear that God's knowledge of men's deeds is in a general sense.

The word together *is stressed. God knows the order He has arranged for mankind in general (together) but in the case of each particular man his destiny can be changed by means of his own free choice amid the possibilities God has arranged for him. The reference to the "heavenly bodies" is to the belief that these have an effect on human life and are therefore God's instruments in determining the order of events. Gersonides cannot disregard the "science" of astrology.*

Furthermore, it is the opinion of our Torah that God never changes, as it is said: "For I the Lord change not" (Malachi 3:6). And Balaam, at a time when he was a prophet, said: "God is not a man, that He should lie; neither the son of man, that He should repent" (Numbers 23:19). And yet we find in the words of the prophets, on whom be peace, that God does repent over some things, as it is said: "And the Lord repented of the evil which He said He would do unto His people" (Exodus 32:14). And it is said: "For the Lord is gracious and repenteth Him of the evil" (Joel 2:13). Now it is impossible to solve this contradiction if we adopt the view that God knows particular things as particulars. But it is easier to solve the contradiction if we adopt the view that God knows things in the manner we have suggested. It follows, therefore, that according to the Torah God knows things in the manner we have suggested.

A further proof is now presented. Sometimes the prophets say that God does not change His mind and yet sometimes they suggest that He does. (Balaam, remarks Gersonides, spoke as a prophet of God at the time of his utterance even though one would not normally quote the heathen Balaam in support of theological views.) There is a contradiction here, but on Gersonides' view it can be resolved. With regard to His general ordering of events God never changes. This order remains always as He has ordained. But as

*part of that order there are possibilities open to man and it must
follow that as a result of man's free choice things may happen which
God did not know beforehand and in this sense it can be said
that He (i.e. His knowledge) changes.*

According to our view of God's knowledge of things the solution
to the problem is much easier. God's foreknowledge does not determine that this event will happen to this man. But God's foreknowledge determines the way things are ordered in general, and this
order includes the possibility of any particular event being determined by human free will. Hence a particular event which God
knows as a *possibility* may not, in fact, happen because man freely
decides that it should not happen. If, however, we adopt the view
that God knows the events of this particular man as a particular man
it must follow that there is change in God's will. And in general we
find nowhere in the words of the prophets, on whom be peace,
anything to suggest that God's foreknowledge is other than we have
suggested, namely, the way rational thought suggests.

*Gersonides here says that since both rational thought and the
teachings of Scripture agree on this matter this is the view which must
be adopted. Gersonides' view is that God knows everything that
can be known but He does not know beforehand how possible
events will, in fact, turn out, for if He did they would not be
possibilities but certainties and man would not then be free. In a
sense, then, Gersonides believes God to be more limited in
knowledge than did traditional Judaism. Reason required him to
say this about God and he did not find it incompatible with Judaism.
Nor for all the strangeness of the idea did the traditional authorities
feel that Gersonides had done more than exercise the freedom
of thought which was part of Judaism.*

Is man free? PART III

The differences between man's will to believe
and the compulsion to believe.

We wish to explain our view in greater detail and solve in the process the tremendous problem with which earlier thinkers have grappled unceasingly. This is the problem of how God's justice in apportioning reward and punishment can be compatible with the fact that all is determined. If justice is somehow compatible with pre-determination, is there a real difference between a determined act done where there is no accompanying sense of force and compulsion and one done where there is a sense of force and compulsion?

The basic problem is how to reconcile God's foreknowledge with human free will. If God knows beforehand what man is to do, how can man be free? And if man is not, in fact, free, how can he be rewarded justly for the good he does or punished for the evil he does? Maimonides, as above, answers that we cannot understand how both can be possible, but since we must nevertheless believe both reason suggests that we simply do not know how God knows. Gersonides, as above, sees no other way out than to say that God only has foreknowledge of the various possibilities open to man but has no foreknowledge of how a man will, in fact, behave in a particular set of circumstances. Reason forces him beyond Maimonides, and he sets a limit to God's knowledge. Crescas has a third solution. He attacks the other, the human side of the dilemma. He boldly affirms that man is not really free. Here he considers the difficulties involved in holding such a view. Crescas is the only Jewish thinker of note in the Middle Ages who is a determinist, one who believes that a man's acts are all determined by certain previous causes. In this and other matters Crescas had a great influence on Spinoza. The first two problems Crescas mentions are: 1) If everything is determined (by God, of course, since He is the Creator) how can He with justice reward or punish man for doing what he cannot help doing? 2) Even if for some reason it is just to reward and punish a man for things he cannot help doing, why does everyone agree that man should not be rewarded or punished for things he does under compulsion e.g. when others force him to carry out certain acts?

Think of the latter question this way: let the good deeds or the sinful acts be the causes, and their rewards or punishments the effects of these determined acts. In such a case it is illogical for any distinction to be made between determined acts where there is no sense of compulsion and determined acts where there is a sense of compulsion. It is not reasonable that rewards or punishments should be the effects in the one case and not in the other. This is illogical since in either case, with or without a sense of being forced, there is no escape from determinism.

Here we have an elaboration of the second difficulty. All acts are determined by God. If, therefore, reward and punishment follow on these acts, even though the reward and punishment are undeserved, they should follow even on acts a man has been compelled to do. The logic of the argument is that if one looks at the acts themselves (one done with a sense of compulsion and the same sort of act without that sense) there is no difference in the two cases since the very same acts have been performed. If, on the other hand, one looks at the amount of free choice in the acts there is again no difference between them, regardless of what a man senses, since he cannot help performing those acts even when he imagines that he is free.

Perhaps we should admit that some distinction can be made between the acts. In the one case, where there is no sense of compulsion, the act can be called a willed act, even though a necessary one, because

there is no sense of inevitability. In the other case, where there is a sense of force and compulsion the act is done without the will, so there is no room for reward or punishment. Yet even if we admit all this, how can I understand assigning reward and punishment for holding religious opinions?

A third difficulty is now stated. Since everyone agrees that there can be no reward and punishment for acts done under compulsion (where there is a sense of compulsion) how can man ever be rewarded for having right beliefs and punished for having wrong ones? He cannot help himself and he has a sense of compulsion to believe what he does.

Our tradition informs us of the severe penalties for false beliefs. The Rabbis speak of them for unbelievers in the Torah, for heretics and those who deny the resurrection. The Mishnah records the names of certain persons who have no share in the World to Come for entertaining false beliefs. Now in this area of religious belief there can be no opportunity for the exercise of free will or choice of any kind for a number of reasons.

Crescas first says that our tradition does state that false beliefs are punishable. He quotes the severe penalties, such as exclusion from the bliss of the World to Come, for people who deny certain basic Jewish beliefs. Now here, he says, the case can only be compared to that of the man who is compelled by others to do certain acts. In matters of belief a man cannot have the sense of free choice he has with regard to the performance of certain acts. To demonstrate that this is so Crescas proceeds to show that a man cannot choose which things to believe.

First, if the will itself is capable of determining belief then any belief one arrives at would have nothing to do with truth since one could believe whatever one wished to believe. Thus if someone so willed he could simultaneously believe two contradictory ideas. This is utter nonsense.

First, says Crescas, if will is all that counts in belief one might believe anything at all. If a man could freely choose what to believe this would mean that whatever a man did choose to believe would be

*a true belief for him. If, then, he wished to believe one day that
two and two make four and the next day that they make five,
both beliefs would be true for him. This is obviously nonsense.*

**Second, if the will is capable of determining belief then the truth
which leads to the will to believe would be in doubt. This must
follow since if there is no doubt in the truth of that which causes
one to will to believe, no effort of the will is necessary. If, on the
other hand, there is doubt in the cause of the belief and we overcome it by an act of will then the doubt is bound to be carried over
to the belief itself.**

*Here is another argument to prove that a man cannot choose what
to believe. There must be a cause for man's choice, a reason for him
choosing this belief rather than that. Now if he chooses to believe
a certain proposition because he feels that it is true, then no
exercise of the will is required. He has seen the truth and that is
the end of the matter. The whole idea of a choice can only have
meaning if he is not sure whether the reason for holding the belief
is a sound one. But if he is not sure, then his choice is to believe
something about which he is not sure and this, too, is nonsense since
to believe something means to be sure of its truth. For Crescas
and for most of the thinkers of the Middle Ages belief meant with
full certainty and without doubt. Thus in the Maimonidean creed
each statement is introduced by "I believe with perfect faith . . ."
But it would seem to be a characteristic of modern man that he
always carries along with him a measure of doubt. His moments of
certainty are likely to be followed by new questions. Yet because
he sees his doubts as coming out of his belief and leading on to
deeper faith, he is a man of faith in the modern mode.*

**Third, it can be proved from another point of view that belief can-
not depend on the will. For if belief means anything at all it must
affirm something objectively as well as subjectively. Whatever is
objectively true cannot be dependent on the will to believe in it.**

*The third argument is that in any event it makes no sense to say
that because a man chooses to believe something it is true for him.
Belief in a proposition means that the proposition is not only true
for the believer but for everyone. It is objectively, not subjectively,*

true. A subjective statement such as "I like cheese cake" expresses no more than a purely personal preference. It does not seek to provide us with any information about things apart from the person making the statement. But an objective statement such as "The moon is a quarter of a million miles from earth" is a statement about a reality outside the person who makes it and would be true even if the person who makes it did not exist. Now anyone who says that he believes something is surely making a statement which refers to something objective and as such this cannot possibly depend on something subjective like the human will.

Having proved that belief does not depend on the will, I argue as follows. Whoever believes something to be true, especially if the belief is arrived at by demonstration, cannot help having a sense of compulsion and a feeling of utter necessity to hold this belief. Since the reason for his belief overpowers him so that he cannot escape it, and since once the truth has been demonstrated it becomes a necessary obligation for him to believe in it, then the obligation to believe in it is so clear and obvious and he feels it so powerfully that it becomes quite impossible for him by nature to believe anything which contradicts his belief. Consequently, this belongs to the category of things in which there is a sense of compulsion and, as we have argued, it is not right for there to be reward and punishment in this area. I cannot therefore understand how reward and punishment can have any application to beliefs.

It follows that a man must believe what he believes. He cannot help believing once he has been convinced of the truth of that in which he believes. His will to believe otherwise is as powerless as it would be if someone forced him to commit an act against his will. But in that case why should there be reward and punishment for beliefs if we have agreed that there can be no reward and punishment for acts a man is compelled to do? In the nineteenth century the American philosopher William James wrote a famous essay on this whole theme entitled The Will to Believe. Crescas has now stated three difficulties: 1) How can there be reward and punishment if everything is determined? 2) If there can be, why does this not apply to acts done with a sense of compulsion? 3) Why are matters of belief not treated under the heading of things done with a sense of compulsion? Then, as now, it was one part of a philosopher's duty to create intellectual difficulties, not for their own sake but as a means of reaching an intellectually more satisfying understanding.

The following can be said to remove these difficulties. First, divine justice always tends to promote the good and the perfect. Now since the good and the perfect need that which encourages men to do good it must follow that the divine justice requires rewards and punishments for men's deeds since these encourage men to do good. The rewards and punishments follow on the deeds like any other chain of cause and effect and by so doing they encourage man's free will to draw near to certain acts and keep far from others. In this way the difficulty of reconciling the divine justice in alloting rewards and punishments for determined acts is resolved.

Crescas' solution to the first difficulty is to argue that when we say that God's foreknowledge determines how men will act this means how they will act under promise of reward and threat of punishment. Crescas here makes a well known distinction between fatalism and determinism. The fatalist believes that man is fated to do certain things and cannot help himself. For the fatalist a thief is bound to steal because it has been so decreed or ordered. But the determinist believes that the thief's acts have not been fated. The thief can choose whether or not to steal and his choice will be determined by such things as the promise of reward and the threat of punishment. What is determined by God's foreknowledge, says Crescas, is not the act but the choice i.e. God knows how the thief will choose and he is not, therefore, really free in his choice, although he is free not to steal. The hope of reward and threat of punishment are means of helping a man to make up his mind and are, therefore, instruments of the good. But, as many of Crescas' critics point out, this still does not really explain how it is just for man to be rewarded or punished for things which are determined by God's foreknowledge.

As for the difference between determined acts where there is no sense of force or compulsion and determined acts where there is a sense of force or compulsion, this can be accounted for as follows. We have explained earlier (and proved it by means of both rational thought and an appeal to Scriptural verses, and this agrees, too, with

Rabbinic statements in a number of places) that the purpose of good deeds is the delight and joy man experiences when he does them. This is nothing else but that the will should find it sweet to do good. This is because God, in His infinite love, desires man to love the good deed. So the will to do good is the nearest approach possible for man if he is to walk in God's ways. It follows that this delight and desire of the soul is the psychological instrument by means of which man is either attached to or detached from God. Consequently, it is right that reward and punishment should follow this as in any other chain of cause and effect. But where the soul has no such desire, when a man senses that his deeds are done under force or compulsion, then there is no soul participation in those deeds. From such deeds neither attachment nor detachment can result since they have been stripped of every psychological motivation. In such circumstances it is not right for reward or punishment to follow on the deeds. This is the way in which the distinction can be defended.

Crescas now deals with the second difficulty. God, he says, loves good and hates evil and He wishes man to be like Him in this. The hope of reward and the threat of punishment can help to promote the love of good and the hatred of evil and they are therefore given not so much for the sake of the acts themselves as for the promotion of the right spirit, the right psychological attitude. But where a man is compelled to perform certain acts his own will is powerless and there is no point in seeking to encourage that will by holding out to him any hopes of rewards and any threats of punishment.

But granted that the distinction can be defended, how can the difficulty regarding beliefs be solved? The difficulty is that the promise of reward and the threat of punishment for beliefs cannot have the effect of encouraging men to will to believe and they cannot be an effective cause of beliefs since we have demonstrated that man is not free with regard to his beliefs and that beliefs have nothing to do with the will.

Crescas now turns to the third difficulty. If the purpose of reward and punishment is to encourage the proper attitude toward good and evil, if it has a psychological purpose, how can it apply to beliefs where, as Crescas has demonstrated, the will is powerless?

(Crescas adds here a lengthy side argument which we have omitted because it is highly technical.)

The answer to the difficulty is this. We have explained that the will has nothing to do with belief, and that the believer feels himself compelled to believe as he does. From which it follows that there is no other way out of the difficulty than to attribute free will and choice to that which is attendant on belief. This is the joy and pleasure we have when we attain to the beliefs God has graciously given us and the effort to arrive at the truth. These matters, without doubt, do have an association with free will and choice.

Crescas replies that reward and punishment are not for the beliefs themselves but for the pleasure one has in holding them and for the effort a man takes to reach his belief i.e. for the way in which he approaches the evidence for and against. A man's will does have something to say in the fields of pleasure and effort and here he can be helped by hopes of reward and threats of punishment.

Now that we have studied three approaches to the problem of free will and God's foreknowledge, it might be remarked here that most thinkers who have considered this extremely difficult subject come to the conclusion that neither Gersonides nor Crescas have advanced really helpful solutions. In each case while reason has tidied up the dilemma by limiting either God's knowledge or man's freedom, a good deal has been lost of the traditional Jewish feeling that God knows all yet man is capable of acting freely. So the most religious attitude would be that of Maimonides who knows enough to know that he doesn't know exactly how God knows, but trusts in His knowing and in man's freedom anyway.

Belief in the impossible

The elements of faith and reason in man's beliefs.

Not every belief leads to happiness. No happiness can result from belief in the impossible. No one doubts that the only type of belief which results in happiness is belief in that which is true, not a belief that a non-existing thing exists or that an existing thing does not exist.

Only a true belief can satisfy the mind and promote happiness.

Since this is so it is right to ask: How can we know that whatever we believe in is true in itself, so that we can believe in it with perfect faith, or that it is not true, so that we can reject any belief in it? If we reply that the answer is to be found by means of rational thought this would mean that philosophical knowledge is superior to faith. But that would contradict all that we have postulated earlier. This is a serious problem and we must try hard to offer a solution.

Albo has said earlier in his book that faith is superior to philosophical knowledge. Philosophy may not lead man to the truth but faith will. But since Albo has also stated that not every kind of faith is valuable, only faith in that which is true, one cannot say that something is true merely because one believes it to be true. There must be some means of testing our beliefs. If we test them by using rational thought and so arrive at our conclusion, it would seem to make rational thought the judge of belief and therefore superior to it. Albo's reply is that faith in tradition should not be rejected merely because rational thought finds it impossible. Since it can be true, we should rely on tradition which states that it is true, and here faith has the deciding voice and is superior to reason. But reason has a role to play nonetheless. Reason can show us that certain things are real impossibilities, that they cannot possibly be true and cannot therefore be believed in.

We notice that there are two kinds of impossibility. Some things are impossible in themselves so that we cannot imagine even God making them possible. For example, the whole is greater than a part of it and the diagonal of a square is greater than one of its sides. Now we cannot imagine that even God can make a part equal to the whole; or a diagonal of a square equal to one of its sides; or the angle of a triangle equal more than two right angles; or two contradictory propositions true at the same time of the same subject; or the affirmative and the negative true at the same time of the same thing in the same relation. It is impossible for tradition to make us believe in any such impossibilites. It is impossible for our senses to testify that these or similar things are possible since our minds cannot imagine them. For this reason it is not right to believe such things, just as it is impossible for tradition to demand that we believe that God can create another being like Himself in every respect. For that would involve one being a cause and the other its effect so that they would not be similar in every respect.

Albo's distinction is between a logical impossibility and a physical impossibility. Modern thinkers have elaborated on the thoughts presented here. God cannot do the logically impossible, not because there are limits to His power, but because there are no such things. When we ask God to do the logically impossible we are not, in fact, asking Him to do anything at all. The words we use are nonsense words. In the examples Albo gives, the words whole and part are mutually exclusive so that they cannot mean the same thing; the diagonal of a square and one of the sides of a square cannot by definition refer to the same thing. The point about two contradictory propositions is that these can be true of the same thing at different times but not at the same time. The propositions that there is no one at the North Pole and there is someone at the North Pole can obviously both be true at different times but not at the same time. The point about the affirmative and the negative is as follows. It is possible to affirm that this water is hot and to negate by saying that this water is not hot if one is thinking of different quantities of water or of the same quantity of water at different times. It is also possible both to affirm and negate the same thing at the same time if one is thinking of different relations. For example, one can say the water is hot in relation to ice, but is not hot in relation to fire. But one cannot both affirm and negate the same thing at the same time in the same relation. Albo's final example deals with the old philosophical problem: Can God create another like Himself? If He can then He would no longer be the one God. If He cannot there are limits to His power, there is something He cannot do. The answer is that by definition a created being could not be like God who is uncreated so that we are talking nonsense when we ask if God can do this. Nonsense does not make sense because we tag the name "God" to it.

There is another kind of impossibility and this we can imagine God making possible. This is the kind of thing only impossible according to the laws of nature. Such things, though impossible according to the laws of nature, are not impossible for the Creator. Examples are: the resurrection of the dead; the possibility of a human being living forty days and nights without food and drink; and other such marvelous things which are impossible according to the laws of nature. Since the mind can imagine them, it is possible to believe in such impossibilities.

Physical impossibilities are only impossible for us but there are no limits to God's powers. To put it another way, odd acts do occur. Very odd acts don't occur normally, but that is not to say that it is altogether impossible for them to occur.

We can, therefore, argue that anything the mind can imagine (even though it is impossible according to the laws of nature) can be believed to have existed in the past, to be existing in the present, or to come into existence in the future. This is especially so of some-

thing which experiences testify is so, even though the mind denies its existence through a failure to understand its cause. An example is the magnetic attraction for iron. The mind, unable to grasp its cause, denies its existence. Since, however, experience testifies that it is so and the thing can be imagined by the mind, even though the mind cannot fathom its cause, it is undoubtedly true.

Albo says that we must not think that a thing is impossible simply because the mind does not understand its workings. The mind cannot understand how a magnet works but our experience tells us that magnetic force is a reality. Albo's distinction is between things the mind cannot possibly conceive (logical impossibilities) and the things the mind can conceive but cannot understand (physical impossibilities).

Similarly, those marvelous things to which the senses testify, such as the revival of the dead by Elisha during his lifetime and after his death; a human being remaining forty days and nights without food and drink, as did Moses and Elijah; the Divine Presence resting upon Israel, and other such marvels to which the senses testified at some time in the past and which the mind can imagine even though it cannot explain them, these and similar things can be believed in and are within the power of the Infinite Being.

Albo concludes that the Biblical miracles can be believed in because they are not logical impossibilities and, as in the case of the magnet, there is the testimony of former generations that they actually happened. The British philosopher Hume agreed that what is really involved in the acceptance of a miracle alleged to have happened in the past is whether the people testifying to it are reliable. For Elisha see II Kings 4:32-37; 13:21. For Moses and Elijah see Exodus 34:28; II Kings 19:8.

Jewish mysticism

MYSTICISM IS difficult to define accurately. But the mystical approach in religion generally refers to an especially acute awareness of the divine and, in religion as we know it in the Western world, a particularly keen awareness of God. Mysticism in this sense is sometimes described as religion in its most intense form. The religious mystic is the person who has a profound experience of God.

Jewish mysticism has a long history. Numerous passages in the Bible (the dream of Jacob, Genesis 28:10-22, Moses at the burning bush, Exodus 3:1-15; Moses and the elders, Exodus 24:9-11; the vision of Isaiah, Isaiah 6:1-8 and Ezekiel, Ezekiel, 1:1-28 and many others) have a strong mystical quality. Similarly there are a number of mystical passages in the Talmud. The following is the best known and typical of the elusiveness of meaning in passages which speak of mysteries beyond the normal human ken: Our Rabbis taught: Four men entered Paradise while still alive. They were: Ben Azzai, Ben Zoma, Elisha ben Avuyah and Rabbi Akiva. Rabbi Akiva said to the others: When you reach the stones of pure marble (which look like water) do not say "water, water" because Scripture says "He that speaketh falsehood shall not be established before mine eyes" (Psalms 101:7). Ben

Zoma gazed and died and of him Scripture says: "Precious in the sight of the Lord is the death of His saints" (Psalms 116:15). Ben Azzai gazed and became insane and of him Scripture says: "Hast thou found honey? eat as much as is sufficient for thee, Lest thou be filled therewith, and vomit it" (Proverbs 25:16). Elisha ben Avuyah broke off the shoots (the plants and trees growing there). Rabbi Akiva left there in peace (Tractate Ḥagigah 14b).

In this passage it is fairly obvious that "entering Paradise" refers to some kind of mystical speculation the details of which we do not know. The same applies to the marble stones and the shoots. In all probability these are metaphorical expressions but we do not know now what it is that they refer to. The passage also points to the dangers in mystical speculation. Ben Zoma died in ecstasy (or so it would appear). The experience was too much for him. Ben Azzai, as the proverb says, "ate more than his fill." He was a young man and not yet ready for the experience, which unbalanced his mind. Elisha ben Avuyah (called in the Rabbinic literature *Aḥer*, the other one) became an apostate i.e. he left Judaism altogether. Only the mature Rabbi Akiva emerged in safety. Later Jewish teachers discouraged young men from studying the mystical books. According to some authorities these should not be studied before the age of forty.

But although there are many mystical ideas in the earlier sources the Jewish mystical system is chiefly contained in what is known as the *Kabbalah*. This is not a *book* but a body of mystical teaching which arose in the twelfth century, although many of its ideas can be traced back to the earlier periods. The "father of the *Kabbalah*" is said to be the French teacher, Isaac the Blind of Posquières (twelfth to thirteenth centuries). The word *Kabbalah* means *tradition* i.e. because its teachings were believed to have been handed down from generation to generation back to Moses himself. Its practitioners are known as *Mekubbalim*, *Kabbalists*. It can hardly be accidental that the *Kabbalah* arose at a time when some of the greatest of the Jewish philosophers had been teaching. What seems to have happened is that the philosophers, in describing God in the most abstract of terms, had made religion seem remote and apart from the living concerns of men. The *Kabbalists*, while accepting the philosophic view that God is Spirit and can only be defined in the most refined spiritual terms, tried, at the same time, to sound the note of a more vital and vibrant faith. How they tried to do this will, it is hoped, become clearer from the following selections.

Jewish mysticism is highly speculative. It is an exceedingly complex series of contemplative exercises on God's nature in His relationship to the created world. Although we have spoken of it as an experience, the *Kabbalah* is, in fact, a system of thought. Some of the *Kabbalists* devoted the whole of their intellectual life to this "science" (*hokhmah*) as they called it. While the philosophers tended to discuss the question of God's providence in a detached way, the mystics believed that a more vivid and intimate picture of ultimate reality had been revealed by God and this revelation was to be found in the classics of the *Kabbalistic* literature. From this point of view the *Kabbalah* afforded its devotees with food for speculative thought but afforded them, too, the certain attainment of truth, a certainty that was desperately needed after the breakdown in Jewish life which followed on the Expulsion from Spain. One of the results of this new interest in the *Kabbalah* was the reinvigoration of Jewish observances. For the *Kabbalists* every detail of the Jewish practices mirrored some aspect of the divine reality and this tended naturally to invest the *mitzvot* with cosmic significance, serving also as a means of bringing color and poetry into Jewish religious life.

The most important of the *Kabbalistic* works is the Zohar (the word means *light*). This is a lengthy mystical commentary to the Five Books of Moses together with a number of supplementary parts. The work is written mainly in Aramaic but there are passages in Hebrew. The work is attributed to the second century teacher, Rabbi Simeon ben Yohai, a pupil of Rabbi Akiva, and is said to be the disclosure of the special mysteries revealed to him by God. In addition to the Zohar proper there is a work known as the New Zohar (*Zohar Hadash*) and one known as The Perfections of the Zohar (*Tikkuné Zohar* or *Tikkunim*). The Zohar was brought to the attention of the learned Jewish world by Moses de Leon in Spain in the thirteenth century. Most modern scholars hold that Moses de Leon was, in fact, the author of the Zohar, though, as with the *Kabbalah* generally, many of the ideas do go back to an early period.

In the sixteenth century, after the expulsion from Spain, the city of Safed became one of the four holy cities of Palestine and a famous center of mystical activity. The two great names among the Safed mystics are Moses Cordovero (1522-1570) and Isaac Luria (1534-1572). The latter really developed a new mystical system of his own (the Lurianic Kabbalah, as it is frequently called). He wrote very little himself but his teachings were recorded by his disciples. (Luria was called *Ha-Ari*, The Lion, and his disciples were called The Lion's Whelps.) The most prominent of these was Ḥayyim Vital (1543-1620). Among other famous *Kabbalists* influenced by the Safed school are: Elijah de Vidas, author of *Reshit Ḥokhmah* (The Beginning of Wisdom), a pupil of Cordovero; Eliezer Azikri, author of *Sefer Ḥaredim* (The Book of God-Fearing Men), a member of the Safed circle; Isaiah Horowitz (c. 1565-c. 1630), author of *Shené Luḥot ha-B'rit* (Two Tablets of the Covenant); and Joseph Ergas (1685-1730), author of *Shomer Emunim* (Guardian of Faithfulness). A somewhat later author is Alexander Süsskind of Grodno (d. 1794), author of *Yesod v'Shoresh ha-Avodah* (The Foundation and Root of Divine Worship).

The eighteenth century saw the rise of the Ḥasidic movement. This was a mystical movement founded by Israel Baal Shem Tov, The Master of the Good Name (d. 1760), differing from the earlier *Kabbalah* in extending its teachings to the masses rather than the chosen few. This movement produced a host of well-known spiritual masters. The Baal Shem wrote nothing himself but his ideas are to be found in expanded form in the writings of his disciples and their disciples.

Mystical writings in the older tradition were produced as late as the twentieth century. A particularly noted exponent was the late Rabbi Abraham Isaac Kook (1865-1935) the first Chief Rabbi of Palestine.

Elijah's mystical prayer

The relation of the infinite God to the finite world.

Elijah began to praise God saying: Lord of the universe! You are One but are not numbered. You are Higher than the highest. You are the mystery above all mysteries. No thought can grasp You at all. It is You who produced the Ten Perfections which we call the Ten *Sefirot*. With them You guide the secret worlds which have not been revealed and the worlds which have been revealed, and in them You conceal Yourself from human beings. But it is You who binds them together and unites them. Since You are in them, whoever separates any one of these ten from the others it is as if he had made a division in You.

This mystical prayer contains all the basic mystical ideas of the Zohar. It is recited to this day by many devout Jews at the beginning of the prayers of the day and has been printed in many prayer books. "One and not numbered" means that the term "one" when applied to God is not like the numeral "one" after which there is a "two" and a "three." God is unique, totally different from everything else in the universe. The meaning may also be that He is not numbered in the Sefirot. Sefirot means "numbers" but they are also called here Tikkunim, "Perfections," which is also the name given to this section of the Zoharic literature—The Tikkunim or the Tikkuné Zohar. With this term we come to the basic theory of the Zohar. The Sefirot are understood to be ten emanations which come from God.

Nothing a human can say about the Én Sof is really meaningful. However, God manifests Himself to His creatures, though in a "hidden" way, within the Sefirot. About the Sefirot, which is to say about how God interacts with His creation through the interplay of these ten emanations, Jewish mysticism has a lot to say. God as He is in Himself cannot be known at all. This utterly transcendent aspect of God is called Én Sof—That which is without (én) limit (sof).

The Zohar also believes in the existence of higher worlds, spiritual worlds hidden from human beings and revealed worlds such as our own. One cannot really understand our world except in terms of the others, with which it is intimately connected. More, the Bible must be understood not just in reference to our world but in terms of all the levels of creation.

The point about separation is as follows. The great danger of the Zoharic system for Jewish belief is that the Sefirot might be treated as gods. This would mean that there are ten gods which would be as serious an offense against pure Jewish monotheism as it is possible to imagine. Hence the Zohar stresses that there is only the One God and He unites all the Sefirot in His Being so that to separate any one from the others and give it a life of its own would be blasphemy. It suggests, as it were, that there is division and multiplicity in the One God Himself.

These Ten Sefirot follow the order of long, short and medium. You, O God, control them but there is none to control You, neither above nor below nor in any direction. You have prepared garments for them, from which souls fly into human beings. You have prepared many bodies for them, called bodies in relation to the garments by which they are covered.

Nine of the Sefirot are divided into groups of three. One of each is long, representing God's mercy, another short, representing His judgment (somewhat like our terms long suffering and short-tempered) while the third is medium, representing a harmonizing principle between judgment and mercy. The further idea contained here is that there are, as it were, two sets of Ten Sefirot, the one higher in spiritual rank than the other. These are said to be like garments to the body. The garment Sefirot are lower in spiritual rank than the body Sefirot. Human souls are said to be derived from the garment Sefirot.

This is the order they follow: *Ḥesed* **(Lovingkindness) is the right arm;** *Gevurah* **(Power) is the left arm;** *Tiferet* **(Beauty) the torso;** *Netzaḥ* **(Victory) and** *Hod* **(Splendor) the two legs;** *Yesod* **(Foundation) the extremity of the body, the holy sign of the covenant;** *Malkhut* **(Sovereignty) the mouth, which we call the Oral Law. The brain is** *Ḥokhmah* **(Wisdom), the inner thoughts.** *Binah* **(Understanding) is in the heart and of it we say: "The heart understands." Regarding these latter two Scripture says: "The secret things belong unto the Lord our God" (Deuteronomy 29:28).**

Nine of the Ten Sefirot are now named. They are listed in three groups of three. As we shall presently see, the last group is somewhat different from the first two. As the individual Sefirot are mentioned we hear of the seven which are, as it were, the manifestations of the divine emotions and actions before these descend to control the worlds. Lovingkindness (Ḥesed) is represented by the right arm of the body. The Zohar sees the human body as a representation of spiritual realities in the realm of the Sefirot, the world of God's first manifestation. (The Zohar does not, of course, intend to suggest that God has physical organs.) Right in most languages represents the stronger and the more correct. God's lovingkindness is both stronger and more abundant than His judgment. Power (Gevurah) is represented by the left arm. Beauty (Tiferet) is the harmonizing Sefirah (singular of Sefirot.) It preserves the balance between Lovingkindness and Power. Harmony is beautiful and beauty harmonious. This is the central Sefirah and is represented by the torso. That is the first group of three. The next two Sefirot, Victory (Netzaḥ) and Splendor (Hod), are two further principles of right and left and are represented by the two legs, one on either side. Foundation (Yesod) is a further harmonizing principle. It is represented by the organ of generation and is therefore called "the sign of the holy covenant" i.e. of circumcision. That is the second group of three. The next Sefirah is Sovereignty (Malkhut), the source of God's rule over His creatures. This is represented by the mouth which gives expression to the thoughts and intentions of men. Similarly this Sefirah gives expression of God's intentions in their final form and is also called The Oral Law which explains The Written Law. But now the enumeration shifts to what are generally considered two more elevated Sefirot. These are: Wisdom (Ḥokhmah), represented by the brain, and Understanding (Binah), represented by the heart, i.e. the inner life. These, because they have to do with God's inner life, as it were, are very secret and even further from any human comprehension than the previous seven. Perhaps some mystery is implicit in this particular order for it is not easy to determine what is intended.

The elevated *Keter* **(Crown) is the Crown of Sovereignty and of it Scripture says: "Declaring the end from the beginning" (Isaiah 46:10). It is the skull upon which the** *Tefillin* **are placed. From within it is** *yod, hé, vav, hé,* **which is the way of emanation. It provides the water for the tree, its arms and its branches, just as a tree grows when it is watered.**

The most elevated Sefirah of all is the divine will and is known as Crown (Keter). It is represented by the crown above the head or by the skull upon which man wears his Tefillin. It is the beginning of God's creative processes but envisages the end of all of these processes. Its inwardness is represented by the Tetragrammaton, the four letter name of God, when each of its letters has been spelled out in full. (All the letters of the Hebrew alphabet, according to the Zohar, represent profound spiritual realities.) The four letters of the name spelled out in full are yod, hé, vav, hé and, in Hebrew, these have ten letters. Hence the figure of a kind of inner power in Crown from which the other nine Sefirot and Crown itself emerge (emanate). The Zohar is trying here to grapple with the great mystery of how God's creativity begins, how, as it were, the first impulse to create (from which all else ultimately follows) has its origin. The "tree" and its "branches" are metaphors for the Sefirot even as in the previous paragraphs the human body was used as its symbol.

Lord of the universe! You are the Cause of causes, the Ground of grounds, who waters the tree by means of a spring and that spring is as the soul to the body by which the body survives. In You there is no likeness or image of anything within or without.

Nothing either "within" (among the Sefirot) or "without" (in the worlds below them) can be compared to God. God is not the Sefirot. He, like a soul, animates them and gives them identity. So they disclose Him and show Him in His working. But the Sefirot are not God.

You created heaven and earth and produced in them sun, moon, stars and planets and upon earth trees, plants, the Garden of Eden, animals, birds, fishes and human beings in order that through them the upper worlds can be known and it can be known how the upper and lower worlds are controlled and how the upper and lower worlds can be recognized.

In Zoharic teaching everything we know and see is evidence of God's manifestation in the universe. All things are thought of as reaching back from this, the lowest world, to ever higher worlds to to the world of the Sefirot and from there to God Himself.

No one can know anything about You. Apart from You none is unique and there is no unity apart from You in the upper and lower worlds. You are known as Lord of all there is. Among all the *Sefirot* each has a special name by which the angels are called. But You have no special name for You fill all names and You are the Perfection of them all and when You remove Yourself from them all names remain as body without soul.

God as He is in Himself is utterly unknown and cannot be known. Only the Sefirot, His manifestations, have names. That is critical because being is detected and described by its name ("What's your name?") but God cannot be known and ultimately no special name is adequate to Him as He truly is. The Zohar understands all the names of God to be the names of God as manifested in the Sefirot, not of God as He is in Himself. The angels sometimes carry the name of the Sefirot. Jewish mysticism took the old tradition of angels quite seriously though what the angels were understood to be could be varied.

You are wise but not by means of a known wisdom. You understand but not by means of a known understanding. You have no known place except to make known Your power and might to human beings and to show them how the world is controlled by judgment and mercy, which are righteousness and justice, according to the deeds of men. Judgment is the same as Power. Justice is the same as the Middle Pillar. Righteousness is the same as Holy Sovereignty. "Just Measures" are the same as the Two Pillars of Truth. The "Just Hin" is the same as the Sign of the Covenant. It is all for the purpose of demonstrating how the world is controlled. But it does not mean that You have a known righteousness which is Judgment and a known Justice which is Compassion. You have none of these qualities at all. Blessed be the Lord for ever. Amen, Amen.

God is wise but His wisdom cannot be known just as He Himself cannot be known. Note how mysticism and philosophy seem quite close here as elsewhere. God has no "place" i.e. no special occasion when He is just and another when He is merciful but all is done through the Sefirot each of which has its "place." Some further names for the Sefirot are now given. Judgment (Din) is the same as Gevurah (Power) and is also called Tzedek (Righteousness). Justice (Mishpat) is the same as Tiferet (Beauty) and is also called "The Middle Pillar" (the harmonizing principle is in the center). It is also called Raḥamim (Compassion). Although Tzedek belongs to Gevurah its final manifestation is in Sovereignty (Malkhut). Scripture refers to "just measures" and a "just hin" (the name of a measure in Biblical times). That is not simply to give a rule concerning the market place. Rather it teaches something about the higher worlds as well. The two are always involved with one another. Here "just measures" are said to refer to Victory (Netzaḥ) and Splendor (Hod), the Two Pillars of Truth (because they support Tiferet, Beauty, which, as the harmonizing principle, is also called Truth). All this is extremely complicated but is typical of Kabbalistic symbolism which is worked out in profuse and very ingenious detail. Every law of the Torah, much less every verse about God could now be seen as revealing truths about the heavenly realms. More important, every Jewish practice, no matter how trivial its observance might seem, had a cosmic importance. What one did in this world had an effect on the world of the Sefirot. The Commandments not only made a better human order but were beneficial to the divine order as well.

The soul of the Torah

What the Torah is truly trying to teach.

Rabbi Simeon said: Woe to the man who says that the Torah merely tells us tales in general and speaks of ordinary matters. If this were so we could make up even nowadays a Torah dealing with ordinary matters and an even better one at that. If all the Torah does is to tell us about worldly things there are far superior things told in worldly books so let us copy them and make up a Torah of them. But the truth is that all the words of the Torah have to do with lofty themes and high mysteries.

For the Zohar everything in the Torah has a profound mystical meaning. All the simple tales really are there to tell us, if only we learn to penetrate beneath the surface, of high secrets about God. For the Kabbalists the Torah is not to be taken literally, but is to be studied as a series of mystical texts. Thus the Biblical references to Abraham, for instance, are to the Sefirah Lovingkindness (because Abraham represented this on earth and practiced lovingkindness); the references to Isaac are to Gevurah; and the references to Jacob to Tiferet.

Come and see! The upper and lower worlds are equally balanced. Israel is here down below, the angels are up on high. Of the angels up on high Scripture says: "who maketh thy angels spirits" (Psalms

104:4). The angels are spirits but when they come down to earth they have to be clothed with the garments of this world. If they are not clothed in something like the garments of this world they cannot remain in this world and the world cannot contain them. Now if this is true of the angels how much more so is it true of the Torah, which created them and created all the worlds, all of which only survive because of the Torah. The Torah could not be contained in the world were she not clothed in the garments of this world. Consequently, the Torah stories are only the garments of the Torah. Whoever imagines that the garment is the Torah herself and not other than the Torah, may he expire and have no share in the World to Come. This is why David says: "Open Thou mine eyes, that I may behold wondrous things *out of* Thy Torah" (Psalms 119:18), namely, from that which is beneath the Torah's garments.

According to the Zohar God created the angels and the world by means of the Torah. In this sense Torah must be understood as something like a fundamental principle or idea. The verse in Psalms speaks of ruḥot, generally translated "winds." But the word can mean "spirits" and is evidently so understood by the Zohar. If, then, even angels have to assume some kind of bodily form if they are to come into this world (otherwise they would be too high for this material world) how much more so the Torah herself. (Hebrew has no neuter and the mystics take the feminine gender of Torah seriously.) Therefore the divine mysteries cannot be imparted directly but have to assume the garments of worldly language and worldly tales so that the Torah can have some connection with this world. (The Zohar believes in angels but holds that the human form the angel assumes when it descends to earth is only, as it were, the disguise of the spiritual being called an angel. The Hebrew word malakh literally means messenger.)

Come and see! There are garments which all can see. So when fools see a man clothed in what seems to them to be a beautiful garment they do not bother to look any further. But the garment is given its significance by the one who wears it and the body of the wearer is given his significance by the soul. So it is with regard to the Torah. The Torah has a body. These are the precepts of the Torah which are called "Bodies of the Torah." This body is clothed in garments, namely the worldly tales of the Torah. The fools only look at the garment that is the Torah tale and do not know of anything more, not bothering to look beyond the garment. Those who know more do not look at the garment, but at the body of the Torah beneath it. But the wise, the servants of the Most High King, those who stood at Sinai, only look at the soul, which is the most significant of all and the real Torah. In the World to Come they will have the privilege of gazing at the soul of the Torah's soul.

The term "Bodies of the Torah" (Gufé Torah) is Rabbinic and really means the main parts of the Torah. But the Zohar takes the word gufé literally as "bodies of." Naturally the Zohar speaks of the Kabbalists in the highest terms. They "stood at Sinai" i.e. their souls were there when the Torah was given and they know the true meaning which is the Torah's soul. But even the Kabbalists are limited by their human nature in this world. In the World to Come they will be taught even higher things and will learn to know the soul of the Torah's soul.

Come and see! Above, too, there is a garment, a body, a soul and the soul of a soul. The heavens and their hosts are the garment. The Community of Israel (the *Sefirah Malkhut*) is the body which receives the soul which is the Beauty of Israel (the *Sefirah Tiferet*) and is therefore in the relationship of soul to body. This soul to which we refer, the Beauty of Israel, is the real Torah. The soul of the soul is the Holy Ancient One (the *Sefirah Keter*) so that all are interconnected.

This is a further mystical treatment of the theme of garment, body, soul and soul's soul. These are present in the realm of the Sefirot. Thus Malkhut is the body, Tiferet (also called The Written Torah i.e. it is the source of the Torah) the soul, and Keter the soul's soul. Another Zoharic name for Keter is the Holy Ancient One because it is the first of the Sefirot.

Woe to those wicked men who say that the Torah is only a mere tale, who look only at the garment and proceed no further. Happy are the righteous who have the proper attitude toward the Torah. Wine can only be preserved in a bottle and in the same way the Torah can only be preserved in its garment. Consequently, one

should only look beneath the garment. Therefore all those matters and all those tales are merely garments.

This is based on the Rabbinic saying about a young scholar: "Look not at the bottle but at what it contains. A new bottle may contain old wine whereas an old bottle may not have even new wine in it."

The mystics obviously shared the philosophers' need to explain the significance of much in the Bible. The philosophers gave deeper meaning to many passages either by saying they were allegories, human qualities given personal form, or poetic ways of putting rational truths. The mystics agreed the stories and poems had a deeper truth. Only they found it in ideas about God and His Sefirot, not in philosophic concepts.

God is unchanging

Why God should act if He is perfect.

We must not attribute any change whatsoever to God. We must not, therefore, believe that anything new happened to Him, God forbid, when He created all things. But He was before anything came into existence and He is after everything has come into existence and He exists constantly without any change or renewal whatsoever. If we imagined that all creatures came to naught this would not involve any change at all in Him.

Cordovero was a tremendously prolific writer. Like other mystics he chose flowery titles for his works. His most famous work is the gigantic compendium of the Kabbalah, Pardes Rimmonim (Orchard of Pomegranates) which he wrote when he was only twenty-seven years of age! Elim is a place mentioned in the Bible at which there were palm trees. The work based on this name is divided into sections called "palm trees" and, the title of the work is therefore "The Great Elim." The problem Cordovero discusses in this section is how to understand the multiple change we observe in the world. These must have their origin in God's will but it is a basic belief of the Kabbalists, as of the philosophers, that God's will never changes, that God never changes His mind. A human being changes his mind because of new circumstances presented to it but since God is the Author of everything, there are no new circumstances for Him. This notion of perfection as necessarily static began to

change only in the nineteenth century. Today it seems much easier
to think of ultimates in dynamic terms so that growth and change
are a part of the best we know. In any case, note how intellectual
a problem this mystic has set for himself.

Since this is so one might ask: Does not the name of God as the
Cause of causes suggest, God forbid, that He suffers change since
before He caused them He was not called the Cause of causes?
The same difficulty applies to all the other names of God all of
which refer to His relationship to His creatures.

Any name we give to God suggests that He does something or
functions in a special way, such as the name Cause or Good. But this
would appear to mean that before He functioned in that way and
acquired that name He had not yet wished to function in that
way, and this would seem to suggest that there is change in God.

The truth is that God has neither attribute nor any kind of name.
God never had any name and now, too, He has no name whatsoever
and no attribute of any kind. His being has suffered no change and
will never change.

Cordovero says that, in fact, God cannot really be given any name.
When we do name Him, even as Cause of causes or First Cause,
it is only from our point of view.

From His point of view His goodness would flow even if there were
none to receive it i.e. if there were no creatures at all. No greater
goodness is added to His being because there are now recipients
of His goodness. The idea of God as Cause and Author is always
part of His nature to which nothing is ever added and from which
nothing is ever subtracted. Certainly creatures came into being at a
given point in time but even before that time there was in God the
cause of those effects that were later to come into existence and an
active principle by means of which they were later to be actualized.
This potential was part of His nature. God and His potential are
one and He never changes. The change from potential to actual is
only in creatures, whether they actually enjoy existence or not.
However, the activating principle operates all the time and the

cause is always present even when the effects are only potential. That which God willed when creatures came into being is what He willed before they came into being. For God does not change from having one will to having another and whatever He wills He wills constantly. For His will never changes. His will is always with Him and He is with His will from the emergence of His will and for ever.

Cordovero's basic solution to the problem is that God is always the same perfectly good, ever active Being but the changes are in the recipients. He willed from the beginning that this or that would happen at a given time.

When it is said that the world suffers change, for instance that the world will last for six thousand years and be destroyed for one thousand, or the idea of the Jubilee and the world's renewal and that the moon's light will be as great as the sun's, and so forth, it does not mean that there is any change in God's will, that He changes His mind, God forbid. Whatever He willed from the beginning that He wills for ever. But God's will belongs to the mystery of His influence and His self revelation by means of the Crown, the will of wills. There is to be found His purpose of being good to all. When, however, He uses the various means of achieving this purpose He becomes remote from them so that these means change in accordance with the changes to be found among the creatures beneath Him. The closer these are to Him the better they are able to receive His goodness and last forever and become perfect. The change is not in Him, God forbid, and not from His point of view but in them and from their point of view because they are remote from Him.

Cordovero elaborates on the solution. There are references in the earlier Jewish sources to the world undergoing a change of status at certain times. For instance some of the Rabbis say that after the world has existed six thousand years it will be destroyed by God and then recreated and renewed as a much better world. This period of renewal is called the Jubilee and it was believed that in the perfected world at that period the moon's light will be as powerful as the sun's. Many of these notions conflict, of course, with the modern scientific picture of the universe, but Cordovero's argument is not affected. What it all amounts to is that the belief of the emergence of a perfect world in the Messianic age seems to suggest a change in God, that until that age He willed one kind of existence for man and in that age a different kind of existence. Cordovero's reply is that the goodness and perfection of the Messianic age is, as it were, present all the time but men cannot yet make it their own. When they succeed in doing this the Messianic age will, in fact, be here. The change is in people not in God. He introduces the Kabbalistic idea of the Crown. As we have seen in the previous passages this is the source of God's will. Now, says Cordovero, at this highest stage there is only an unchanging will for good. But this has to be expressed in creative activity and the Kabbalah holds that as God's will unfolds to bring creatures into being it becomes, as it were, further from its source in God since God is One and unchanging whereas creatures are, by their very nature, many and changing. But again beneath all the changes for and in creatures there is only the unchanging good will of God. The Kabbalistic system here shows its intellectual usefulness in the Middle Ages. The static perfection is explained by the Én Sof. The active, dynamic aspects of God's creativity are found in the Sefirot, but these are distant from their source.

Now we long and hope for His nearness. We wish to be attracted by those means which bring us near to Him until we are able to receive His goodness when it is abundantly revealed. That will enable the world to be renewed for good to its uttermost limits.

The Messianic hope is that the whole world will come closer to God and hence nearer to His goodness. Here again mysticism is closely linked with living according to God's law and not to mere experience or speculation.

The matter can be compared to the sunshine which provides a very sweet and clear light. But those who have weak eyes can only bear the sun's light if they see it through many veils which weaken the light and keep it from them except to the extent that they are able to stand it. Once their eyes have been healed, however, the veils can be progressively removed so that they can come closer to the sunshine and take pleasure in its light. Now the closer they come the more the sun's light is renewed and the more it changes; however, the change is not in the sun but only in connection with their own changed condition and nature. It is exactly the same with regard

to the renewal of the world, the renewal of its creatures and of human comprehension of the divine, not that there is any change whatsoever in God's will.

A man with weak eyes needs sunglasses (as we would say nowadays) and insofar as the sun's light is screened from him he cannot have any enjoyment of its full splendor. This is a very interesting way of explaining God's goodness. It is there all the time but men have to progress to ever greater heights in order to enjoy it. The changes are not in God but in their own character. Mysticism teaches men to see what they are normally blind to or perceive only dimly.

CHAPTER 23

God's withdrawal

The mystery of God's creation of the universe.

Know that before there was any emanation and before any creatures were created a simple higher light filled everything. There was no empty space in the form of a vacuum but all was filled with that simple infinite light. This infinite light had nothing in it of beginning or end but was all one simple, equally distributed light. This is known as "the light of Én Sof."

These extremely difficult meditations are those of R. Isaac Luria but were written down by his disciple R. Ḥayyim Vital. Vital wrote a number of books expounding his master's theories and they are the major source books of the Lurianic Kabbalah. The Zohar, we have seen in an earlier passage, holds that the world was created by means of ten emanations, the Ten Sefirot. The Lurianic Kabbalah considers what happened even before these were caused to be emanated. This is more than an effort to explain the ancient puzzle of how creation came to be. By this teaching Luria wants to explain the continuing relation between the Infinite and the finite, and to lay the groundwork for explaining how evil came into the good God's creation. Én Sof (without limit) is, as we have seen, the Kabbalistic name for God as He is in Himself, i.e. apart from His self-revelation to His creatures.

Two things have to be said before studying this passage. First, although the Kabbalists use terms like "before" and "after" in describing Én Sof's creative activity, they really think of these processes as occurring outside time altogether. (It is, of course, impossible for us to grasp this idea of existence outside of time, but for the Kabbalists, as for some of the philosophers, time itself is a creation.)

Secondly, all the illustrations of a vacuum, an empty space, a line and the like are seen by the Kabbalists as inadequate pointers to spiritual realities. They never tire of warning their readers not to take them literally as if there really is, for instance, a space in God. God is outside time and space. Similarly, terms like above and below are only figurative. Unless this is appreciated the whole subject becomes incredibly crude.

There arose in His simple will the will to create worlds and produce emanations in order to realize His perfect acts, His names and His attributes. This was the purpose for which the worlds were created.

In the "simple light of Én Sof" there emerged a will to create. (Note the way in which it is avoided saying that Én Sof willed directly, because this is considered as touching on a mystery too deep for human understanding.)

Én Sof then concentrated His being in the middle point, which was at the very center, and He withdrew that light, removing it in every direction away from that center point.

In the Lurianic Kabbalah creation is only possible by God withdrawing Himself. The logic is simple. Where there is God there cannot be any creatures since these would be overpowered by His majesty and swallowed up, as it were, into His being. This idea of Luria's is known as Tzimtzum (withdrawal).

There then remained around the very center point an empty space, a vacuum. This withdrawal was equidistant around that central empty point so that the space left empty was completely circular. It was not in the form of a square with right angles. For Én Sof withdrew Himself in circular fashion, equidistant in all directions.

If the "empty space" left after Én Sof's withdrawal were to be depicted as a square this would suggest that after the withdrawal

Én Sof *is nearer to the center at some points more than others whereas the circumference of a circle is equidistant from the center at all its points.*

The reason for this was that since the light of *Én Sof* is equally spaced out it follows by necessity that His withdrawal should be equidistant in all directions and that He could not have withdrawn Himself in one direction to a greater extent than in any other. It is well known in the science of mathematics that there is no more equal figure than the circle. It is otherwise with the figure of a square, which has protruding right angles, or with a triangle or with any other figure. Consequently, the withdrawal of *Én Sof* had to be in the form of a circle.

Én Sof *is infinite and it cannot, therefore, be said that He is nearer one point than another. The great difficulty here lies in the whole concept of a limitation of the Limitless.*

Now after this withdrawal of *Én Sof* (which left an empty space or vacuum in the very center of the light of *Én Sof,* as we have said) there remained a place in which there could emerge the things to be emanated, to be created, to be formed and to be made. There then emerged a single straight line of light from His circular light and this came in a downward direction, winding down into that empty space.

Even after God's withdrawal there has to be something of Én Sof *in the empty space otherwise nothing could exist there (nothing can exist without God's power). Therefore a line of light (figuratively speaking, of course) is said to wind downward into the empty space. The figure is of a kind of deep hole in the center down into which the line of light winds itself. In the empty space left after* Én Sof's *withdrawal, the various worlds emerged. In the Kabbalah there are four main worlds, corresponding to the four infinitives mentioned. These are: 1) The World of Emanation (the realm of the Sefirot); 2) The World of Creation (lower in degree than the former); 3) The World of Formation (lower in degree than the first two); 4) The World of Action (or Making), the world as we know it, the physical universe (or, as many Kabbalists understand it, the spiritual source or counterpart of this world of ours). All four worlds are seen as emerging in the empty space or vacuum.*

The top end of this line derived from *Én Sof* **Himself and touched Him, but the bottom end of this line down below does not touch the light of** *Én Sof.*

This is, of course, a figurative way of expressing the thought that somehow finite existence is connected with God's Infinity.

By means of this line the light of *Én Sof* **is drawn down to extend itself down below.**

By means of the line there is something of Én Sof *in the empty space to sustain the beings God creates.*

Into that empty space He caused to emanate, He created, He formed and He made all the worlds.

Note the reference to the four worlds—emanate, created, formed, made. The last three are based by the Kabbalists on the verse: "Every one that is called by My name, and whom I have created for My glory, I have formed him, yea, I have made him" (Isaiah 43:7).

Before the emergence of these four worlds *Én Sof* **was One and His name One in a wonderful, mystical unity of a kind beyond the comprehension even of those angels nearest to Him. For the mind of no creature can comprehend Him since He has neither place nor limit nor name.**

God as He is in Himself (Én Sof) apart from the four worlds cannot be comprehended by His creatures. Only God can know Himself.

CHAPTER 24

God's glory in the synagogue

What it is that gives the synagogue its special sanctity.

It belongs to the respect one should have for the Synagogue that one should not raise one's voice there to call someone or for any other reason. For it is a custom for those who live in a royal palace never to raise their voices in the king's presence but only to speak softly. Now Naḥmanides advised his son to behave modestly and never to raise his voice except when studying the Torah or praying since the whole earth is full of God's glory. This belongs to the practice of humility and it is good to follow this advice at all times. Certainly when a man stands in the house of the King of the universe, where the Divine Presence rests, it is proper to behave in this modest way. By so doing he acknowledges that he stands in awe of the Divine Presence and he carries out the duty of being in awe of the Sanctuary.

Elijah de Vidas wrote his Reshit Ḥokhmah *(Beginning of Wisdom) as a moralistic work in the spirit of the Kabbalah, as a preparation for those who wish to study the Kabbalah. The Kabbalists believed that a man should not engage in this study unless he is prepared to lead an especially holy life and books such as this sought to offer him guidance. Jewish mysticism offered no escape from the life of commandment. To the contrary, the mystic was expected to be more scrupulous in his observance since he knew how every act affected the higher world.*

*The passage quoted here is part of the section on the Fear of God.
The Divine Presence of God is called the* Shekhinah *(the word used
in the Hebrew original of this passage, from the root* shakhan, *to
dwell). De Vidas believes that the Presence of God is in the
Synagogue and other sacred places in, as it were, a more
concentrated form. The idea that deity was to be found in certain
hallowed spots on earth is very old. The prophets who taught
that the whole earth is full of God's glory were seeking to rid
people of this primitive notion that God is only present in certain
places. De Vidas is aware of the difficulty and his solution seems
to be that while God is everywhere, His holiness is, as it were,
especially strong in the Synagogue and other holy places. Naḥmanides'
letter to his son has been quoted in full in this book in the
section on Jewish Ethics.*

**The reason we are obliged to stand in awe of the Sanctuary and
other holy places is because dread should be present whenever the
holy is encountered. As we have explained earlier it is in this connection that it is said of Jacob our father, on whom be peace; "And
he was afraid, and said: 'How full of awe is this place! this is none
other than the house of God' " (Genesis 28:17). Onkelos paraphrases
this as: "This is no ordinary place." This is because those who are
in the king's presence are in awe of him.**

*Onkelos was a second century convert to Judaism who translated
the Five Books of Moses into Aramaic. His translation is not a literal
one and he frequently offers a paraphrase of the verse. The state
of awe described in this whole passage has been acutely analyzed
by the modern religious thinker, Rudolf Otto, in his book
The Idea of the Holy.*

**Now although the whole earth is full of His glory yet because of
His love for us He concentrates His Divine Presence among us as
He used to do between the staves of the Ark and the place of the
Holy of Holies in the Temple. Of the Tent of Meeting we also find
that once it had been finished Scripture says: "And Moses was not
able to enter into the tent of meeting, because the cloud abode
thereon, and the glory of the Lord filled the tabernacle" (Exodus
40:35). Similarly, of the Temple, when Solomon brought the Ark**

into the Holy of Holies, Scripture says: "The priests could not stand to minister by reason of the cloud; for the glory of the Lord filled the house of the Lord" (I Kings 8:11). The Synagogue, too, is filled with the light of the glory of the Lord. Even though we see nothing it is essential to believe this with perfect faith.

The Rabbis say that God concentrated His Shekhinah between the staves of the Ark, the holiest spot in the Temple. The word for concentration is the word Tzimtzum which we have noted in our examination of the Lurianic Kabbalah. There it chiefly means withdrawal, but this is really only a further meaning of the term. If God is, as it were, concentrated in a particular place, this involves His withdrawal, as it were, from other places. De Vidas remarks that we cannot see the glory of God in the Synagogue with our physical eyes because what is concentrated there is spiritual and cannot be grasped by the senses. But, he says, faith assures us nonetheless that it is there. Here again the mystic sees what the ordinary man misses.

It is right for us to argue from the lesser to the greater, namely, from the respect we are obliged to pay to the aged we can see how much more we are obliged to respect the Synagogue. For we have explained earlier that the respect we are obliged to pay to the aged is because of "Who can see the Holy Beard on High and not be abashed in its presence?" In the same way we should say: "Who can see the splendor of the Divine Presence, which is called Glory, and not be abashed?" If you retort that you cannot see it then you are lacking in faith. In similar fashion the Zohar says that if a man opens his eyes when reciting the Eighteen Benedictions he insults the Divine Presence and has no awe of the Divine Presence.

This is typical of the mythological nature of a good deal of Kabbalistic thinking and explains the opposition to the Kabbalah on the part of many Jewish thinkers. The Zohar explains the command to respect the aged on the grounds that the beard of the old man is a kind of reflection of God's beard. This is a very strange concept and the Kabbalists themselves never tire of stressing that if taken literally it is greatly offensive to the religious taste. The Holy Beard represents the spiritual reality of God's mercy. Just as the strands of the beard are attached to the face, the spiritual powers of mercy flow from God's wisdom. (The Kabbalists would say that these spiritual entities when they unfold and come down into this world assume the physical form of a beard.) The argument from the lesser to the greater is that the Shekhinah is a much stronger manifestation than the beard so that in the Synagogue, when the Shekhinah is present, man should certainly be in a state of awe.

On good deeds

The proper way in which man should
carry out a mitzvah.

I wish first to record all the conditions required if the *mitzvot* **are to be carried out properly in order to be acceptable to our King and Creator, blessed be He, and in order that we should not be ashamed when we enter the World to Come.**

Eliezer Azikri's book is a classification of all the precepts (mitzvot; singular, mitzvah, a command, a good deed) and a guide to their performance in the spirit of the Kabbalah. One or two technical observations have been omitted in this translation.

The Kabbalists believed that every good deed done by man on earth becomes part of a beautiful spiritual garment for his soul in Paradise. Hence Azikri says that if a man heeds his counsel and performs the mitzvot *properly he will not be ashamed in the World to Come.*

The first condition is that we should carry out each *mitzvah* **with the intention of fulfilling our duty to God. Rabbi Isaac Alfasi, Maimonides and Nahmanides all agree that intention is required in carrying out the** *mitzvot.*

The three teachers mentioned all wrote works on Jewish law and their decision in these works is that it is not only necessary to do the mitzvot *but to know that one is doing a* mitzvah. *Proper intention is so important that Azikri makes it his first condition*

The second and third conditions are to perform the mitzvot **with love and fear of God. As Rabbi Simeon ben Yoḥai said: "A precept performed without fear and love is no precept."**

The saying of Rabbi Simeon ben Yoḥai is in the Zohar of which work Rabbi Simeon was believed to be the author. The mystics attached great significance to the love and fear of God.

The fourth condition is to carry out the mitzvah **with great joy. For every** mitzvah **is a divine gift and the reward for its performance is in proportion to the joy with which it is performed. The saint and** Kabbalist, **our teacher Rabbi Isaac Ashkenazi, may the memory of the righteous be for a blessing, told this secret to a trusty friend: that all he had comprehended (for to him were opened the gates of wisdom and the holy spirit) was because he used to rejoice with limitless joy whenever he carried out a** mitzvah. **He observed that this thought was contained in the verse: "Because thou didst not serve the Lord thy God with joyfulness, and with gladness of heart, over the abundance of everything" (Deuteronomy 28:47). The meaning of "over the abundance of everything" is that one should rejoice over the** mitzvot **more than over every worldly delight, more than over gold and fine gold, precious stones and pearls.**

Rabbi Isaac Ashkenazi is R. Isaac Luria to whom reference has been made earlier in this book. He is said here to have attributed all the Kabbalistic revelations afforded him to the fact that he rejoiced greatly when carrying out the mitzvot. Note that the first four conditions for doing a mitzvah properly have to do with the inner attitude of the doer. One might expect this of a mystic. Yet there is nothing especially mystical in any of the four conditions.

The fifth condition is that the whole of the mitzvah **should be carried out, not only a part of it. For it is written: "**All **the commandment which I command thee this day shall ye observe to do" (Deuteronomy 8:1). Rashi in the name of the Midrash comments on this: "Once you begin to perform a** mitzvah, **see that you finish it." The Rabbis say further that if a man begins to perform a** mitzvah and he does not finish it that man's rank is taken away from him, for a *mitzvah* is only called after the one who finishes it. However, if he cannot possibly finish it this should not prevent him from doing as much as he can.

Rashi is the famous eleventh century French commentator. "All the commandment" is said to mean: "Do all of it if you can, not only part of it leaving the rest to someone else."

The sixth condition is to take great care when performing a *mitzvah* to do it properly by attending to all the necessary details.

The details involved in the performance of the mitzvot, e.g. that a scroll of the Torah has to be written in a special way, are very important for the Kabbalists for they represent powerful spiritual realities in the "upper worlds."

The seventh condition is to run to do the *mitzvah*, as it is written: "I will run the way of Thy commandments" (Psalms 119:32).

A man should go out of his way to carry out the mitzvot. He should run to find opportunities of doing good, not simply wait until the opportunity comes to him.

The eighth condition is that a man should do the *mitzvah* himself if he can and not get someone else to do it for him. As the Rabbis say: "It is better to do a *mitzvah* oneself than to arrange for a deputy to do it." The *Amoraim* used to make preparations for the Sabbath themselves.

The Amoraim were the great Palestinian and Babylonian teachers in the Talmudic period (the word means interpreters). The Talmud tells us that although they had servants they would prepare the Sabbath lamps and even cook some of the meals themselves because it is a mitzvah to prepare for the Sabbath and they did not wish to delegate it to others.

The ninth condition is to carry out that *mitzvah* which first presents itself before carrying out any others and not to leave it to one side while turning to do another. As the Rabbis say: "It is wrong to pass over one *mitzvah* in favor of another."

The tenth condition is that one should not carry out two or more *mitzvot* simultaneously for one may not be capable of paying proper attention to more than one *mitzvah* at a time. As the Rabbis say: "It is wrong to do the *mitzvot* in heaps."

One should not heap the mitzvot together but do one at a time so that complete attention can be given to each.

The eleventh condition is to have respect for the *mitzvot*. With regard to the *mitzvah* of covering the blood of a bird that has been killed for food, it is said that the covering must be done by hand and not with the foot for this would be an insult to the *mitzvah*. By analogy this principle is to be extended to all the *mitzvot*. We find in the Midrash: "Rabbi Simeon ben Yoḥai said: 'The Holy One, blessed be He, says: Pay respect to the *mitzvot* for they are My deputies and a person's deputy has the same standing as the person himself. If you honor the *mitzvot* it is as if you honor Me. But if you insult the *mitzvot* it is as if you insult Me.' "

See Leviticus 17:13.

The twelfth condition is that one should not allow a *mitzvah* to become sour but as soon as the opportunity presents itself the *mitzvah* should be carried out and not left until tomorrow.

If a mitzvah is left without being attended to for too long a period it becomes sour, there is no freshness in its performance.

The thirteenth condition is that one should wait with keen anticipation the opportunity of performing a *mitzvah*.

One should not simply take the mitzvot as they come, but long for the opportunity.

The fourteenth is to adorn the *mitzvot*. As the Rabbis say: "Adorn yourself in God's Presence when carrying out His *mitzvot*. Purchase a beautiful citron, a beautiful tabernacle, a beautiful prayer-shawl," and so with regard to all the other *mitzvot*. The Rabbis said further: "One should be prepared to pay a third more of the price in order to adorn a *mitzvah*."

For the citron (etrog) and tabernacle see Leviticus 23:39-43. The
reference to a third means, for example, that if an ordinary Torah
scroll costs $600 and one more beautifully written can be obtained
for a higher price one should be prepared to go up to $800
for the better scroll.

The fifteenth condition is to be very energetic in carrying out the
mitzvah. **If a** *mitzvah* **is such that it has to be carried out during the**
day it should be done early in the morning. The Rabbis derive
this from Abraham of whom it is said: "And Abraham rose early
in the morning" (Genesis 22:3). The Rabbis comment: "From this
we learn that the energetic perform the *mitzvot* **at the earliest op-**
portunity." Similarly, if a *mitzvah* **has to be carried out at night it**
should be carried out at the beginning of the night.

This is not to be confused with the twelfth condition. Here even if
he carried it out later he would not be putting it off since it is a
mitzvah which can be carried out at any time during the day.
But it is still correct to do it as soon as possible in order to
demonstrate one's eagerness to do God's will.

The sixteenth condition is that a man should try his utmost to carry
out the *mitzvot* **as part of a group and not on his own. The reward**
of a *mitzvah* **is greater if the** *mitzvah* **is carried out by a number of**
people acting together. The Rabbis say that in Temple times one
priest handed the blood of the paschal lamb to another priest and
he to another and so on until it reached the priest who sprinkled it
on the altar. This was done to give as many people as possible the
opportunity of participating in the *mitzvah.*

When people work together for the good, they encourage one
another. And Judaism is not just the religion of individuals but of
the whole People of Israel. Mysticism might lead to isolation and
concern for self. Jewish mysticism never forgets the importance
of joining with the Jewish community.

The seventeenth condition is that a man should not do a *mitzvah*
without it costing him anything, but he should pay well to do it
without complaining of the cost. This will help to remove the spirit
of uncleanness.

A good deed done without it costing anything is of less value than one for which sacrifices are required. The Kabbalists believe that every good deed produces more holiness in the world and hence helps to remove the spirit of uncleanness and evil. That made their way of life external and activist, not withdrawn and passive.

CHAPTER 26

ISAIAH HOROWITZ: SHENÉ LUḤOT HA-B'RIT,
"TWO TABLETS OF THE COVENANT," PART IV, ASARAH ḤILLULIM

The highest form of worship

The ways in which man should serve God.

To engage in holy worship, the worship of God, is to humble one-self in His Presence, to run to serve Him and carry out all His com-mands. Worship involves man's humility before God for all the goodness He has bestowed upon him from the day of man's forma-tion until the time his intellect matures. For He has done all this in mercy and without any favor from man. If one is expected to be grateful to human beings for any good they do, even if it is unin-tentional, how much more should one be grateful to the Divine Presence, which never ceases from bestowing good upon man.

Serve the Lord with gladness by reflecting on His great love. God desires to love the children of Israel, so He has lifted us up from the dustheap and brought us near to His service and to His Torah. Serve ye the Lord our God!

Blessed is He! He has created the people of Israel for His glory, separated us from those who are in error, given us His Torah and planted eternal life in our midst. He has chosen us from all peoples. He loves us and wants us and has exalted us above all languages.

He has sanctified us, calling us by His great and holy name. Serve ye the Lord your God with joy and with good heart as you recall God's love in all the goodness He has given us.

Fear the Lord your God and serve Him with the kind of service a faithful servant gives. Serve Him by day and by night, at all times, in every hour, every moment, every period. Serve Him with speech, with thought, and with the hidden thoughts of the heart. Serve Him as if His worship were always new and fresh and serve Him with a heart on fire, not as one half asleep but as one strong as a lion desiring to do His will for its own sake. Also let your heart be glad when you avoid wrong-doing by keeping the negative precepts, and say: "I am quite capable of doing this wrong thing but what can I do if my Father in Heaven has ordered me not to do it." For it is man's heart that the All-Merciful wants and He searches all hearts. Serve the Lord with all your heart and pour out your heart like water in God's presence. Be as far as you possibly can from the performance of the precepts in a routine manner without the heart being in them. Be more than two thousand cubits distant from this. Every command should appear to you as if you had only been given it recently, today or yesterday.

It is the way of the righteous, the servants of the Lord, to increase their humility in His presence and their worship of Him the more good He gives them. The proof of this is from tithing. If God gives a man ten, the tithe is one; but if God gives him a hundred, the tithe is ten so that the reward of the man who gives only one is great whereas the one who gives only nine and a half will be punished. If a man has no son he has no obligation to carry out the precept of circumcision. If he is lame he has no obligation to go on pilgrimage. If he is sick he cannot carry out any precept. But those who are able to carry out these precepts must do so. We are therefore obliged to consider God's goodness to mankind in general, His goodness to our people in particular, His goodness to our family in particular, and His goodness to each individual in particular, that we might appreciate how great is His love for us. Let us go in the King's way not turning aside from the right or the left and let us be His servants. Let us praise the Lord for He is good and His goodness endures for ever. To him alone will we give thanks. Furthermore, happy is the man who fears that any goodness God gives to him should not be to reward him in this life in order that he will be lost in the World to Come. Let us serve Him in love without thought of reward and not because of fear of punishment if we do wrong. Let us accept in love both good and evil, accepting both rejoicing and trembling.

Your Creator thinks of you and knows what is good for you. Therefore whatever happens to you, give thanks unto Him. Accept your sufferings in love and with gladness and serve God more than is demanded of you. A man once saw a saint who had an injured leg and said to him: "I am sorry for you that you have an injured leg." The saint replied: "I am grateful to my Creator that the injury was not to my eye," and he gave thanks to God.

Walk in God's ways. Know Him in all your ways. Make no movement unless it be for God's glory. See nothing, hear nothing, go nowhere, stand nowhere, sit nowhere, think nothing, do nothing, hint at nothing, unless it be to worship Him. Want nothing unless it is His will, seek nothing unless it is to seek His desire, rejoice in nothing unless it is for His service and find pleasure in nothing but Him. The rule is, lift neither hand nor foot, move neither eyelid nor mouth and think no thoughts except for God alone.

O my soul, bow down to the dust and be humble before God. Be modest in dress and in conduct. Always be afraid that your service of God is less than adequate. Always recall your sins and transgressions. Let the good which comes to you always seem too much and the trouble you take too little in proportion to what is really fitting. Despise the little good you do when measured against that which you ought to do.

Reflect on God's greatness and on your own smallness. Have God always before your eyes and do not rebel against your Maker, who sees you. Bless the Lord. Let His praises be in your mouth by day and by night. Appear before Him constantly that He may accept your prayers and inscribe you in the book of pardon and forgiveness. Pray to Him continually to put it into your heart to understand, to hear, to learn, to teach, to keep and to do all the Torah.

Since prayer is the service of the heart let us stir ourselves to know which is the gate of Heaven through which prayer ascends. First of all, think to yourself before you pray: "Who am I, a poor miserable vessel full of shame and confusion, that I should come to offer supplication to the King of kings, the Holy One, blessed be He, before whom the angels tremble, if not by virtue of His great love which He shows to His creatures in that He does not despise communal prayer and that He hearkens unto prayer." Do not allow your tongue to anticipate your heart. Before any word of prayer escapes your lips think of its meaning. When you mention God's name be filled with trembling, dread and fear.

Let the wise hear all this and add to it by concentrating in prayer on the innermost mysteries of which a crown is made for the head of the Lord of Hosts. The saintly and men of deeds used to pray in private and concentrate on the mysteries in their prayers and would reach the stage where the soul strips herself of the body. So powerful would be their spiritual state at that time that they approached the degree of prophecy.

Let all the words of prayer emerge with clarity from your mouth for, God forbid, you can destroy the world by means of one letter. See therefore that you make no mistakes and take care over every word. Let your lips express the words distinctly so that you commit no errors, as if you were counting coins.

This long passage is in the form of a mystical, ethical poem on the highest form of worship. The mystic is encouraged to think only of God not of himself. Our author has a very passive attitude. His chief mood is one of resignation to God's will. In the history of religious thought such an attitude is known as "quietism." However, this is only one side of the coin. It certainly does not follow that our author has abandoned the idea, found in the Talmudic literature, that man is to be a co-partner with God in the work of creation i.e. that God, in a sense, depends on man's efforts if the Divine purpose is to be realized. It should also be noted that, unlike the philosopher, the mystic is not bothered by the intellectual difficulty of why God allows men to suffer. His attitude is one of joyous trust in God and a complete readiness to accept whatever comes from Him in love.

The last two paragraphs require some comment. For the Kabbalists it is not the plain meaning of the prayers which is significant but the hidden mystical meaning. Each word of the standard prayers represents some idea in connection with the realm of the Sefirot. The mystics trained themselves to have these ideas in mind while reciting their prayers. Prayer is not only speaking to God, what the prayers explicitly say, but a long meditation on the Kabbalistic mysteries. It was believed further that the mystic's prayers had an influence on the flow of God's grace. By means of the right words uttered in a spirit of complete devotion God's goodness is brought down to earth, as it were. By the same token an inadequate expression could "destroy the world." Isaiah Horowitz, like the other mystics, believed that it was possible for the mystic so to lose himself in his prayer and worship that his soul became almost disembodied and his experience was not unlike that of the prophet when God spoke to him. It remains to be said that in Isaiah Horowitz's book there are to be found many ideas which he culled from other sources. The book has been described as an encyclopedia of the Jewish religion.

Dialogue on the Kabbalah

The authenticity of the tradition of Jewish mysticism.

SHEALTIEL: First of all I want to ask you, how do you know that there are secrets and mysteries in the Torah? For it is accepted by Jews that Moses received the Torah together with its true explanation at Sinai and he handed it down to Joshua who handed it down to the elders . . . until it was handed down to the sages of Israel of old who wrote down the traditions in the Babylonian Talmud, the Palestinian Talmud, the *Siphra,* the *Siphre,* the *Tosephta* and the *Mekhilta.* We obey these and rely on their words and whoever does not rely on them does not belong among the holy people. But where is it stated in the Gemara that there is, as the *Kabbalists* claim, an inner, secret meaning to the Torah?

YEHOYADA: The Rabbis speak of one who conceals matters which the "Ancient of days" (Daniel 7:13) has concealed. What are these? The secrets of the Torah. They say further that the secrets of the Torah must only be imparted to one who possesses five qualities. So that it is stated explicitly that there are secrets in the Torah. These were known to our Rabbis of blessed memory by tradition and they are: The Creation Story, The Story of the Divine Chariot, and The Book of Formation, as Rashi explains. Regarding this the

Rabbis say: "One should not expound the Story of Creation to two disciples at the same time, and to a single disciple one should not expound the Story of the Divine Chariot unless he is wise and capable of understanding for himself." The *Tosaphists* comment in the name of Rabbenu Tam that by the Story of Creation they mean the Divine Name of forty-two letters formed from the letters of the first two verses of the Bible. Now the manner in which the Name of forty-two letters is derived from the verses and the meaning and function of this Name are matters to be found in the writings of the *Kabbalists,* who had all this by tradition. Nahmanides, in his Commentary to the Torah, writes: "The Story of Creation is a deep mystery which cannot be understood from the plain meaning of the verses. It is only known clearly by a tradition reaching back to Moses our teacher, on whom be peace, who received it from God Himself. Those who know the secret must keep it secret." The Ritba writes: "The Great Thing means the Divine Chariot. The reference is to the chariot on high at which the prophets never gazed but whose secret is known to the masters of truth." Rashba gives the same explanation. From all of them it can be concluded that the Story of Creation and the Story of the Divine Chariot are the secrets of the Torah and the divine science which goes back by tradition to Moses our teacher, on whom be peace, who had it from God Himself. This embraces the topics in the Book of Formation which we now have in print. You know full well the powerful scope of these great men in Talmudic learning for the whole house of Israel relies on their Talmudic commentaries. The Rabbis also remark in the Midrash: R. José ben Ḥanina said: The Holy One, blessed be He, said to Moses: To you will I reveal the reason for the red heifer (Numbers 19), but to others it is a statute without reason. From this it follows that Moses did reveal to others the reasons for all the other precepts. Now all this must refer to the science of the *Kabbalah* for this explains the Torah mysteries and the reasons for the precepts and the secrets of the Story of Creation and the Story of the Divine Chariot which have come down to us by tradition from our teachers reaching back to the ancient sages of Israel, the Talmudic Rabbis.

SHEALTIEL: You are quite right and have proven that there are mysteries and secrets in the Torah and that these were known to the

Rabbis who called them the Story of Creation and the Story of the Divine Chariot. But it does not follow from this that the opinions of the *Kabbalists* are identical with those mysteries and secrets of the Torah. Maimonides, of blessed memory, was a great sage and an expert in the whole of the Talmudic literature. He has explained to us in his *Strong Hand,* in the first four chapters of the work, the true meaning of the Story of Creation and the Story of the Divine Chariot.

YEHOYADA: If Maimonides, of blessed memory, had claimed that he had received his explanation by tradition from his teachers then we would have been uncertain as to which of the holy teachers we should follow—the tradition of Maimonides or the tradition of the *Kabbalists* which is in accord with the views of Rashi and the *Tosaphists* and the other commentators we have mentioned. But Maimonides does not, in fact, claim that he has a tradition in this matter but has arrived at it by the exercise of his own mind. As he himself admits in the Introduction to Part 3 of his Guide for the Perplexed, where he says that all his explanations of the Story of Creation and the Story of the Divine Chariot and the secrets of the Torah were not received by him as tradition from his teachers nor were they divinely revealed to him, but he arrived at them all purely by exercising his reasoning powers. It is consequently possible that the matter can be otherwise, the opposite true and the real meaning quite different. This is the gist of what he himself says. How can one therefore accept the doubtful views of Maimonides and reject the certain views of the *Kabbalists,* views which they present to us by testifying that they had received them from their teachers in a tradition going back to the *Tannaim?* Furthermore, Maimonides' explanation has been rejected. All the commentators reject it with both hands. Rabbenu Nissim, of blessed memory, writes: "Maimonides wrote what he wanted to write but if only he had not written it!" The sage and philosopher R. Shem Tov b. R. Shem Tov writes: "Our teacher Moses (Maimonides) produces weak and false arguments. He claims that from the day Israel was exiled from its land there was not found anyone as learned as Aristotle in these matters. The reason why Maimonides thinks evil thoughts all day is that he imagines that there is no wisdom apart from the wisdom of those men (the Aristotelians). It was this which led him to say that the Divine Chariot seen by Ezekiel and Isaiah (which we are obliged to treat as a great mystery) is no more than a small part of Aristotle's learning. This is clear to anyone who takes the trouble to read carefully all the chapters of his book, The Guide for the Perplexed, and examines them paragraph by paragraph and word by word. He tries so hard to get the sense of these men's learning that he even goes so far as to suggest that whatever Ezekiel, on whom be peace, comprehended was known to the majority of Christian, Arabic and Greek thinkers and that they knew it better and in a purer form than Ezekiel, on whom be peace." Many other thinkers write that it is impossible to identify Aristotle's physics and metaphysics with the Rabbinic Story of Creation and Story of the Divine Chariot as does Maimonides, and they proved it from the words of the Rabbis. What the Rabbis intended by the Story of the Chariot and the Story of Creation are matters not to be attained by philosophical reflection but only by means of the science of the Kabbalah, of those who fear the Lord and think on His name, the true sages and masters of the Torah from which alone all these and all other perfections come. A proof of this is that no sage in the natural sciences of the nations ever attained the degree of being able to create anything, but Rava created a calf and R. Zéra a man by means of the Book of Formation. This is the gist of what they say. The truth is that many hold to ridicule Maimonides' explanation of Ezekiel's Chariot and the reasons for the precepts Maimonides gives in the Guide and they write that they wished he had kept silent. Consequently, there is no need for us to give any heed to what he says in these matters.

SHEALTIEL: Perhaps the secrets of the Torah, the Story of Creation and the Story of the Divine Chariot refer neither to one nor the other, neither the view of Maimonides that the opinion of our Torah and our prophets are identical with the opinion of Aristotle nor the view of the Kabbalists, but perhaps the real meaning of the topics has been lost during the long period of exile?

YEHOYADA: This is also a claim which cannot stand, for the Book of Formation, The Book of Brightness, The Chapters on the Heavenly

Halls and the Zohar, which are the works the *Tannaim* compiled on the secrets of the Torah, are in our possession by *Kabbalistic* tradition. Even the sect of the philosophers among our people admit that these works were composed by the *Tannaim*. Furthermore we find that in the days of the *Geonim* (the early post-Talmudic teachers in Babylon) the secrets of the Torah were neither lost nor forgotten. Naḥmanides comments on the verse: "This is the book of the generations of Adam" (Genesis 5:1): "Rav Sherira Gaon writes that the sages handed down one to the other the way to tell character by the face and by the lines of the palm. Some of these are referred to in this verse and others in the following verse. One must only hand down the secrets and mysteries of the Torah to one whose character is known to be suitable." This shows that in the days of Rav Sherira Gaon they knew the secrets and mysteries of the Torah. Rabbenu Hai Gaon wrote letters on the subject of the secrets of the Torah to Rav Paltai Gaon. And Rav Ḥamai Gaon composed The Book of Reflection and The Book of Unity. Some of their words can be found quoted in R. Shem Tov's Book of Faith and R. Moses Cordovero's Pardes. There, too, you will find numerous quotations from many Geonim who wrote on the secrets of the *Kabbalah*.

This lengthy imaginary dialogue between a non-Kabbalist, Talmudic scholar (Shealtiel—from a root meaning "to ask" i.e. an inquirer) and a Kabbalist (Yehoyada—from a root meaning "to know") is a defense of the whole Kabbalistic system against the oft-repeated accusation that, in fact, its name was a lie and that there was no tradition (Kabbalah) in these matters. The Rabbis in the Talmud already speak of certain passages in the Bible as being of particular mystic significance, namely the Story of Creation (Genesis 1:1-2; 3) and the Story of the Divine Chariot (Ezekiel 1; compare Isaiah 6). They also refer to the Book of Formation (Sefer Yetzirah) and say that various teachers actually used this book to create a calf or even a man by a kind of white magic! Maimonides, as a rationalist philosopher, could not abide such notions. Since he attached the greatest significance to the teachings of the Aristotelians, he identified the Story of Creation with Aristotle's physics and the Story of the Divine Chariot with his metaphysics. In effect, he tried to turn mysticism into science. Maimonides' authority was great so that the Kabbalists could not simply ignore him but were obliged to try to refute him. Their claim was that the "secrets of the Torah" referred to by the Talmudic Rabbis were the Kabbalistic mysteries (the doctrine of the Sefirot and so forth) and that the Kabbalistic tradition was authentic. Joseph Ergas tries to be fair to both sides but it can be seen that, as a Kabbalist himself, he does tend to "load the dice" in favor of Yehoyada. Historically, the tradition of Jewish mysticism is older than that of Jewish philosophy.

After the Expulsion from Spain and the subsequent hardships in Jewish life the colder, more detached philosophical approach tended to yield more and more to the warmer, more romantic and more comforting mystical approach. One of the authors of this period observed that in times of religious persecution men of simple but intense faith gave their lives rather than be false to Judaism, while many of the philosophical Jews lacked the conviction to give them the courage to be martyrs. In the sixteenth century the great mystical group of teachers around Moses Cordovero and Isaac Luria in Safed exerted an influence far beyond the borders of Palestine. It should also not be overlooked that a good deal of Kabbalistic teaching has to do with the coming of the Messiah and the redemption of the world. Every good deed, it was taught, brought the advent of the Messiah a little nearer by creating more holiness in the world. This was a particularly hopeful and attractive doctrine in times of stress and positive misery. But the rationalistic forces in post-Renaissance Italy were still powerful so that it is no accident that Joseph Ergas, an Italian author, should have to defend, in the early eighteenth century, the claims of the Kabbalah against its rationalistic critics.

CHAPTER 28

ALEXANDER SÜSSKIND OF GRODNO: YESOD V'SHORESH HA-AVODAH,
"THE FOUNDATION AND ROOT OF DIVINE WORSHIP," PART IV, CHAPTER 5

The meaning of the Shema

The thoughts which should be in the mind
when the Shema is read.

The plain meaning of the words *Hear O Israel* has been explained by Abudarham who writes: "This is a form of testimony as if each Jew says to his neighbor: Hear that I believe that the Lord our God is unique in His world. This is why the letter *ayin* of the word *Shema* and the letter *dalet* of the word *ehad* (one) are found written in the Torah scroll larger than the other letters so as to form the word *ed* (witness) to hint at this testimony."

The New Zohar (p. 60a) has this to say: "This verse (Hear O Israel) had meaning when Jacob's sons said it to him (since his name was Israel) or when Moses said it to the people of Israel. But now when everyone says *Hear O Israel,* to which Israel do they address themselves? We have been taught that Jacob our father did not really die and God has sealed him in His precious Throne that he should be a permanent witness for his sons who affirm the unity of God's name, as is fitting, twice a day. So that when they do affirm the unity of God's name they say: *Hear O Israel!* Be thou our witness that we affirm the unity of God's name as is fitting." At that time Jacob avails himself of four wings spread out in all four directions and he ascends to the Holy One on high and blesses Him with seven benedictions. Happy is the father who bore this seed upon the earth and happy the children who crown their father in this manner. At that moment all the heavenly hosts proclaim: "Blessed is His glorious Kingdom for ever and ever." And Jacob is crowned with thirteen rivers of pure balsam and he stands continually over his children like a wall around a city to prevent strong judgments from having any dominion over them.

Still a further meaning is found in the holy Zohar. This is that the word "Israel" refers to God who is called "Israel." For God is called by many names and among these is Isra-el which means "God is right." So that the meaning of the words *Hear O Israel* is as if man is speaking directly to God: "Hear Thou who art called Israel that I believe with perfect and true faith that Thou art the Lord and our God and that Thou art the one Lord." What the Zohar really means here is so very profound who can grasp it? But my purpose is not to reveal mysteries but to explain the meaning of *Hear O Israel* as the Zohar understands it in its plain sense. You now have three possible explanations of the words *Hear O Israel*. Choose whichever you like provided your heart is in it.

And thou shalt love the Lord thy God with all thy heart. When a man recites these words he is obliged to bring into his heart a strong and mighty love for God. This love is a positive commandment for the holy people and the duty is derived from this verse. If a man is easy-going about this, apart from having failed to fulfill his obligation of loving God, he also speaks a lie, God forbid. The strategy for attaining to this love is for man to awaken with great energy all his limbs and his mind together with all his other senses and to prepare himself to bring this tremendous love into his heart. Then in proportion to his effort at demonstrating his capacity to act, his heart will be all the more on fire in great love.

I shall give you an illustration. We notice that when a mother kisses her baby to whom she is attached in her innermost heart she kisses with all her might because of the tremendous love her heart bears the child and all her being goes into the kiss. So it is with regard to man's love for God, may His name be exalted. This is how the holy Zohar puts it: "And thou shalt love"—a man should worship God in love for there is no greater form of worship than the love of God.

R. Abba said: These words of the *Shema* contain all the principles of the Torah because all the Ten Commandments can be found in these words and our colleagues have found them there. Come and see that God loves nothing so much as the man who loves Him as he should. What does this imply? As it is written—*with all thy heart.* This is the gist of the passage. So how can a man fail to set his heart on fire, to bring into it the most powerful sense of the love of God with all his might, as above. This note is enough.

And with all thy soul. Our Rabbis comment: "Even if He takes away your life." Consequently, he should not speak untruths, God forbid. He should depict to himself that he is suffering martyrdom for God's sake.

And with all thy might. The Rabbis comment: "With all thy wealth." Therefore he should not speak untruths but should depict to himself that he is told: "Either bow down to this idol or we will take away all that you possess," but he retorts: "Take all my wealth but I shall not bow down to your idol or worship it." And he should depict to himself that they take away all he has, even a whole chest of gold coins, and leave him penniless, and all because of his love for God may He be exalted.

And these words which I command thee this day shall be upon thy heart. When he finishes the verse he should say to himself: "I accept it upon myself that this love will always be in my heart."

And thou shalt teach them diligently to thy children. He should take this obligation upon himself by saying to himself: "I accept upon myself the duty of teaching my children Thy holy Torah."

The book from which this passage is taken is a guide to prayer. Alexander Süsskind advises his readers on the kind of thoughts they should have in mind when reciting the various prayers. This passage is part of his comments on the Shema. No doubt the Kabbalists did not take literally the idea of Jacob flying upwards on wings. The reference to Jacob on God's Throne is to the ancient belief that the face of Jacob (Israel) was engraved on the Throne. This, too, was in all probability understood in a figurative sense. The second explanation is very beautiful. Jews, the descendants of the Patriarch Jacob, reassure him that they have kept the faith and not departed from his ways.

On prayer

What the Baal Shem Tov holds
important in prayer.

The Baal Shem Tov revealed that although a man should pray with great attachment to God and with love and fear he should nevertheless be humble, too, before God. For it once happened that he prayed together with his disciples with great attachment to God but without humility, and a great prosecution was instituted in Heaven. Only one member of the company prayed with humility and through him they were spared.

The Ḥasidic movement was a mystical movement which arose in the eighteenth century with special emphasis on the value of mystical prayer. The observations in this passage go back either to the Baal Shem Tov, the founder of the movement, or those influenced by him. An important Ḥasidic ideal was for man to be attached to God (called devekut, from the root davak, to be attached) particularly in prayer. This means a kind of constant mystical awareness of God so that the mind is completely centered on Him. The danger of spiritual pride is stressed here. The reference to the "prosecution" is based on the idea that a kind of heavenly court sits in judgment whenever men are in danger of falling into the trap of pride and Satan takes the part of the prosecuting counsel. Such ideas, despite their ethical quality, are too mythological for the modern taste and it is possible that even the Ḥasidim did not take them too literally, understanding them in a figurative sense. Yet stories abound in the Hasidic tradition of the various Rabbis' intervention in heaven to avert a decree of the court on high.

Rabbi Israel Baal Shem Tov said that when a man reads the Torah and sees the light in the letters of the Torah, even though he does not know how to pronounce the words accurately, then God does not mind even if he does not read correctly since his reading is with great love and with a heart on fire. This can be compared to a little child whom his father loves who asks his father for something he wants. Even though the child stutters and cannot express himself properly the father is very glad. Therefore when a man repeats words of Torah with love, God loves him very much and does not mind whether or not he pronounces the words accurately.

The words in the Torah scroll are written without vowels or notation so that unless a man is a skilled reader he will read incorrectly. The opponents of the early Hasidim, the Talmudic scholars, were meticulous in reading accurately. The Hasidim, on the other hand, tended to attach greater significance to the spirit behind the reading rather than technical accuracy. If the letters are illumined i.e. if there is spiritual power behind the reading, this is the main thing. Another Hasidic ideal mentioned here is hitlahavut (from lahav, a flame) which means a burning enthusiasm in which man's heart is on fire with the love of God. The Hasidim were fond of the illustration of the little child because they believed that the simple faith of the good but unlearned Jew is better than all the learning of the sophisticated teachers who were lacking in true faith. It is not surprising that the scholars retaliated by seeking to ban Hasidism, but without much success.

The holy Baal Shem Tov related that it once happened on a certain Day of Atonement a great prosecution was instituted in Heaven. Satan said that he does not speak of wicked men but of God-fearing and perfect men who go to Synagogue each day for communal prayer but who on their way happen to see a wagon laden with timber and stop to bargain for the wood. They are prepared to come to the Synagogue late for the sake of the small amount the seller deducts as a result of their bargaining. All the angels for the defense

were unable to offer any defense but the Baal Shem did produce an adequate defense. True, he said, before they carry out a good deed they are prepared to let it go even for the sake of some small gain. But once they have carried out the good deed they would not sell it for all the money in the world, and this applies even to the very easy-going. As a result of this speech for the defense all the judgments were sweetened.

The Hasidic leaders were greatly concerned with the sufferings of Jews in Russia and Poland. Life was hard. It was difficult to earn a living and temptations were many. Yet the poor Jews still retained their faith. The Hasidic leaders sought to encourage them as when they told tales such as this. The judgments are God's severe decrees but by the good deeds of man, the Kabbalists believed, these can be made sweet instead of bitter. It is a basic belief of the Kabbalists that man's deeds can influence the flow of God's grace, and that their Rabbis had special mystic powers in this regard.

A man should think to himself before he recites his prayers that he is ready to die through great concentration during the prayers. There are some men who have so powerful a concentration in their prayers that if nature were left to itself they would die as soon as they uttered two or three words in God's presence. If a man thinks of this he will say to himself: "Why should I have some ulterior motive or any pride when reciting this prayer?" since he is ready to die after uttering two or three words. And in truth it is a kindness of God that he is given the strength to complete his prayers and remain alive.

Powerful concentration in prayer was the great Hasidic virtue. The idea here is that man can become so immersed in his prayers and so oblivious to his surroundings that his soul can expire in spiritual longing. It is said of one of the Hasidic teachers that he would always place a clock in front of him when he prayed to recall him to the world of time so that he should not lose himself in the realm of eternity.

When a man is at a low spiritual stage it is better for him to pray from the prayer book when, as a result of seeing the words in print, he will be able to pray with greater concentration. But when a man is attached to the world above he is then better advised to close his eyes so that nothing he sees will distract him from his attachment to the world above.

The Kabbalists believed that man cannot always be on the same spiritual plane. His mood fluctuates between the stage of "greatness of soul," when his soul soars into the "upper worlds," and "smallness of soul," when he is earthbound and when all he can do is to concentrate on the plain meaning of the prayers without any lofty spiritual ambitions.

It is essential that man progresses from stage to stage in his prayers. He should not spend all his strength at the beginning of his prayers but should begin gradually until he achieves the stage of great attachment to God in the middle of his prayers. When this happens he can utter the words of the prayers very speedily. Even if he is unable to pray to God with great attachment at the beginning, he should nevertheless utter the words with great concentration and he should try to become stronger little by little until God helps him to pray with great attachment.

Here, too, the idea of spiritual progress in prayer is stressed.

Similarly, when a man falls from his lofty stage while praying, he should still say the words with as much concentration as he can muster and he can then try hard to return to his earlier lofty stage. This can happen frequently. At first a man should attach himself to the words themselves and later he can put his soul into the words. At first he should move his body with all his might in order that the soul might shine forth. As the Zohar says: "When an ember in the fire does not burn one must poke it and it will then come alight." After this he will be able to worship in thought alone without any bodily movements.

In all religions there are to be found men who believe that bodily movements in prayer can awaken the soul and are therefore powerful aids to concentration. The dancing dervishes are a well known example. The Jewish masters of prayer differed in this matter. Some encouraged swaying and bodily movements in prayer, others discouraged these as too external and undignified. Many of the

Ḥasidim advocated vigorous bodily movements in prayer. Some of
them even used to turn somersaults during their prayers, to the
scandal of their contemporaries. The Baal Shem Tov here seems to
encourage bodily movement as an aid to concentration but, as
he says here and later on in this passage, the most superior form
of prayer is when man has risen to such heights that only his soul
is moved, not his body.

It sometimes happens that a man can only worship in the state of
smallness of soul, namely, he does not enter at all into the higher
worlds but thinks only that God's glory fills the whole world and
that God is near to him. At such moments man becomes like a
child whose mind has only a little maturity. Nevertheless, although
his worship is in a state of spiritual immaturity, he worships with
great attachment to God.

The lower stages of prayer also have their value.

At first a man should pray in fear for this is the gateway to God.
He should say to himself: "To whom do I wish to attach myself?
To Him who by His word created all the worlds, who keeps them
in being and sustains them all." He should reflect on God's greatness and exaltedness. Afterwards he can be in the upper worlds.

The way to the fear of God is to contemplate His greatness as
manifested in the universe.

A man may offer his prayers in a miserable frame of mind because
his melancholia has gotten the better of him and he imagines that
he is praying in a state of great fear of God. Similarly, a man may
imagine that he is praying in a state of great love of God and it is
only really due to the fact that he feels sanguine at the time. However, if a man is in the state of loving God and, as a result, shame
falls upon him and he desires to glorify God and to control his
passions for God's sake, then it is good. For only the man who
worships in fear and love is called a worshiper of God. Fear in this
context means that dread suddenly falls upon him, not that he tries
to work himself up into a state of fear, for this would be "the ascent
of the female waters." But true fear is when terror and dread fall upon

him suddenly and because of this dread he does not know where he is and his thoughts are pure so that tears flow of themselves. But if it is otherwise, even if he imagines that he loves God, it is nothing at all. For fear is the gateway to God. Fear is the gateway to God's love. If he is not even in the gate, which is fear, how can he possibly be in love? One in the state we have mentioned is not even a worshiper and he is certainly not at the stage at which fear can fall upon him. He does not worship at all in a manner fitting for a Jew for he only worships in a routine way. He imagines that he worships God with joy, but it is in reality only the joy of hilarity. He should return to God with all his heart and with all his soul.

This is a very important and interesting section. The real fear of God is something God gives to man. Any artificial whipping up of the emotions is "phony." In the language of the Kabbalah it is called "the ascent of the female waters" i.e. an ascent from man to God instead of the "descent of male waters" from God to man. The female is to be wooed by the male, not the other way round. A man who is simply miserable because of his physical needs is not in fear of God nor is the man who simply feels happy in himself a lover of God. Ḥasidism, a movement which stressed the emotions, always had to be on its guard against an artificial sentimentality.

Prayer with great joy is certainly more acceptable to God than prayer in misery and with weeping. The Baal Shem Tov gave the following illustration. When a poor man requests something of the king with weeping the king only gives him some small thing. But when a prince presents with joy a carefully composed praise of the king and asks for something incidentally, the king grants him whatever he asks, even if it is a great thing, as befits men of rank.

A man should not be a spiritual beggar but a spiritual prince.

A man should not say that he will pray with concentration on the Sabbath but not on a week-day. For this is like those servants of the king who only serve the king well in his presence but are less energetic when he is absent. Such are not faithful servants. Man should sense that it is bad for him without the King and he should push past all the guards until he comes before the King. Even though he is not allowed to speak to the King and it is improper for him to be

in the King's presence, yet the King in his compassion will listen to him.

It is easier to pray properly on the Sabbath when there are fewer distractions and there is greater holiness, but man should seek to "break through" to God even on a week-day.

It is sometimes possible to pray only with the soul, that is in thought alone, the body standing still, in order that the body might not become weak through too much effort. It is sometimes possible for a man to pray in love and fear with a heart greatly on fire without any bodily movements, so that it seems to others that he is uttering the words without any attachment to God. It is possible for man to do this if he is greatly attached to God and he is then able to serve God with the soul alone in great and powerful love. This is a superior form of worship and can proceed more speedily and with greater attachment to God than the type of prayer which makes an external impression on the limbs of the body. The *shells* have no means of grasping the type of prayer that is only internal.

According to the Kabbalah the forces of evil in the world are like shells which surround the nut or the fruit. The meaning is that the more inward the prayer and the more spiritual, the less possibility there is of distraction.

The Baal Shem Tov commented on the saying of the Zohar that a man is judged in each heavenly palace and that he is driven out of the palace. He explained it to mean that the words of the prayers are the heavenly palaces for in them thought dwells. When a man prays he proceeds from letter to letter and word to word and if he is unworthy he is driven away, that is to say, an extraneous thought is thrown to him and he is then automatically outside.

This is an interesting example of what is nowadays called demythologizing, of turning descriptions of another world into ideas we can believe because they talk about our world. The palaces are not up there but in man's spiritual life, in his soul. When his soul is attached to God he is there in the palace. When he is distracted and thinks of other things when he recites his prayers, he is automatically outside.

On evolution

The relation of evolution to the orders of
the world of spirit.

The theory of evolution now busy conquering the world is more in accord with life's mystery as understood by the *Kabbalah* than with any other philosophical theory.

The notion that there is an evolutionary path upwards provides the world with a basis for optimism, for how can one despair when one sees that everything is evolving to ever greater heights? When one penetrates deeply to the principle of evolution in an upward direction one discovers that it illumines with the greatest clarity the idea of God. For only He who is Infinite (*Én Sof*) in reality can actualize that which is potentially infinite.

The theory of evolution, now so well-known as a result of recent scientific researches, has revolutionized our thought patterns. This does not apply to the elite, who approach matters logically and reasonably, for they always tended to see things in terms of development, even the spiritual side of existence which is less tangible. For them it is not at all strange to understand by analogy that the material substance of the physical universe proceeds by the same method of development as the spiritual. It is natural for the physical universe to follow the course of development of the spiritual universe, in which no stage is by-passed or left unfulfilled. But the masses have not yet succeeded in understanding evolution as a consistent and comprehensive theory and have been unable to connect it with their spiritual lives. It is not the difficulty of reconciling certain statements in the Bible or in other traditional sources with the theory of evolution that encourages the masses to remain indifferent. It is easy enough to see how the two can be reconciled. Everyone knows that these topics, which belong to life's mystery, are always dominated by metaphor, riddle and hint. Even the ear of the masses is attuned to hearing the brief formula that this or that verse or statement belongs to the secrets of the Torah which are on a higher plane than the simple meaning would suggest. The masses are quite content to accept such a solution and their opinion is in accord with that of the thinkers who assess the high poetical content that is ever-present when ancient mysteries are expounded. The problem is, rather, how to reconcile the whole way of thinking to which the masses have been accustomed (so that everything appears to them to have erupted spontaneously without any development, and which prevents their minds from considering any new ideas) with the new type of evolutionary thinking they now encounter, a type of thinking which is becoming better known and more convincing all the time. For this a great illumination is required which should penetrate to all classes until its ideas appear reasonable even to the most unsophisticated.

Our age demands, therefore, the spread of a much more elevated, broad and idealistic approach. It is impossible for any crude approach to faith to endure once it has become progressively inferior and has clothed itself in coarse sackcloth. Who will come forward to dress pure faith in the splendid garments she deserves, who will place upon her head the pure diadem which befits her high estate, if not the highly gifted, the wise in heart, the holy in feeling and pure in soul, who are planted in the courtyards of the Lord, the Torah scholars devoted to Torah reasoning and Torah study?

The theory of evolution shows that the world has a core of good which is constantly reaching new heights and this is to be seen in man's desires and nature. Human nature and its desires were, in the past, brutish and coarser than they are now and in the future they will be even more refined. In the past, therefore, the Torah and the demands of the ethical life tended more than they do now to thwart natural human desires because there was more evil in human nature then. But in the future a new pattern will emerge so that men will freely demand greater ethical content to their lives and then all will see how pleasant is the good life.

But there is still much dross in the present state of the human will. Because the goodly sparks of the human will desire progress, the dross in man also wishes to enjoy progress, only its freedom to enjoy progress can destroy the world. For this reason the conflict is severe and each group battles for the right as it sees it and is perfectly entitled to do so. The liberals are fighting for the sparks of good in the human will, that these should not be unnecessarily and superfluously enslaved by the past. And the conservatives, who know the splendors of the past, defend bondage to it so that those aspects of the human will which are unsavory should not destroy the noble reconstruction of the world. The great in soul must be the bringers of peace between the two sides by showing each of them its limits.

Rabbi Kook wrote this at the beginning of this century. Were he alive today he would no doubt have written in a less optimistic vein. But basically what he is trying to do is to demonstrate that the theory of evolution is not only compatible with Judaism but is in full accord with the mystical approach to Jewish life of which Rabbi Kook was himself a distinguished representative. He says here that the Kabbalistic view is that God controls His world in the spiritual realm by stages e.g. from Én Sof down through the Sefirot and the four worlds. In this spiritual realm each stage has its place and none is by-passed. Consequently it is not at all surprising to find these spiritual realities mirrored in the physical processes so that evolution proceeds by stages. Furthermore, the Kabbalistic view is that as man progresses, more and more "holy sparks" are released from evil's control and this will go on until the Messiah comes. Very skillfully Rabbi Kook weds this to the evolutionary theory and applies it also to man's moral life. The highest moral order is where man freely chooses the good and Rabbi Kook believed that there was evidence that this was already happening. Men are more refined, less barbaric and less cruel than they used to be. Consequently, the ethical demands of the Torah are far less in the nature of unpleasant duties imposed from above and far more in the nature of a free response. In the future, Rabbi Kook believes, this will be even more true. He is not disturbed by the apparent and well known contradictions between the Genesis account of creation and the theory of evolution for, he says (and here, too, he speaks as a Kabbalist), it has always been appreciated that the creation narrative in Genesis belongs to "the secrets of the Torah" and should not therefore be understood literally. It might be mentioned that Rabbi Kook's thought on evolution has many parallels with the thought of the famous modern French religious thinker Teilhard de Chardin.

Glossary

Amoraim: the post-Mishnaic teachers in Palestine and Babylon whose views are recorded in the Talmud

Baal Shem Tov: "Master of the Good Name" i.e. one who could use the name of God to perform miraculous acts of healing; name given to the founder of the Ḥasidic movement, Israel ben Eliezer (d. 1760)

ben: "son of"

Binah: "Understanding," one of the *Sefirot*, representing God's reflection in His creative activity

En Sof: "The Limitless," God as He is in Himself, completely unknowable

Gaon, plural **Geonim:** "Excellency," a head of one of the Babylonian academies from the sixth to the tenth centuries C.E.

Gevurah: "Power," one of the *Sefirot*, representing God's sternness and judgment

Ḥasidism: from ḥasid, "saintly," the revivalist movement which arose in Poland in the eighteenth century

Ḥesed: "Lovingkindness," one of the *Sefirot*, representing God's mercy

Hod: "Splendor," one of the *Sefirot*, representing God's splendor and glory

Ḥokhmah: "Wisdom," one of the *Sefirot*, representing God's wisdom in His creative activity

ibn: Arabic equivalent of *ben*, "son of"

Kabbalah: "tradition," the Jewish mystical system

Kalam: "Speech," the Arabic medieval philosophical system

Keter: "Crown," the highest of the *Sefirot*, representing God's will

Kiddush: "Sanctification." The hymn of praise recited over a cup of wine on Sabbaths and Festivals

Malkhut: "Sovereignty," one of the *Sefirot*, representing God's rule over His creation

Mekubbalim: the Kabbalists

Midrash, plural **Midrashim:** Rabbinic commentaries to the Bible

Mishnah: "Teaching," the summary of Jewish teaching compiled by Rabbi Judah the Prince at the end of the second century C.E.

mitzvah, plural **mitzvot:** a commandment, a good deed

musar: "instruction"; the Musar movement, a pietistic movement founded in nineteenth century Lithuania by Rabbi Israel Salanter

Mutakallimun: the Arabic teachers of the Kalam

Netzaḥ: "Victory," one of the *Sefirot*, representing God's control of His creation

Rabbenu Tam: famous French Talmudist, grandson of *Rashi*

Rashba: Rabbi *Sh*elomoh *b*en Adret, Spanish Talmudist (1235-1310)

Rashi: Rabbi *Sh*elomoh ben *Y*itzḥak, famous French commentator to the Bible and Talmud (1040-1105)

Ritba: Rabbi *Y*om *T*ov *b*en Avraham Ishbili, Spanish Talmudist of the fourteenth century

Rosh Hashanah: the New Year festival

Seder: "Order," the home service on Passover eve

Sefirot, singular **Sefirah:** "Numbers," the ten "instruments" or "emanations" by means of which God engages in His creative activity

Shekhinah: "The Divine Presence." Also one of the *Sefirot*, *Malkhut*

Shema: "Hear" (O Israel), Israel's declaration of faith recited twice daily, Deuteronomy 6:4-9

Tiferet: "Beauty," one of the *Sefirot*, the harmonizing principle

Tefillin: "phylacteries," boxes containing Biblical verses and worn during prayer

Tosaphists: the French commentators to the Talmud in the 12th and 13th centuries

Tzimtzum: "Withdrawal," God's withdrawal from Himself into Himself in order to leave room for the world to emerge

Yesod: "Foundation," one of the *Sefirot*, representing the binding principle in the divine realm

Yom Kippur: Day of Atonement